The S'

My Life ar

-

Wenhaston

Jessie Emmeline Ellis
(maiden name Roberts)
1896-1991

Mother of Dr. Jack Roberts Ellis
BSc (Hons), Ph.D
and Heather Phillips M.B.E

Printed by

Leiston Press Ltd

Masterlord Industrial Estate

Leiston

Suffolk

IP16 4JD

Telephone Number: 01728 833003

Email: glenn@leistonpress.com

Web: www.leistonpress.com

Published by ELS Press, 2017

ISBN 978-1-911311-30-0

Contents

Introduction

Heather's mother Jessie aged 18

Jessie's memories were written during her 91st and 92nd year. She had broken her hip and was unable to do much housework or attend to the garden, so she was getting bored. Her daughter Heather suggested that she might like to put pen to paper about her long life. She wrote it all by hand on any paper around, so there is no actual complete document. It was typed some years ago, and that has formed the basis of this book.

Jessie lived all her life on Blackheath in the village of Wenhaston in Suffolk. She was born, married, had her two children, and died there. The text of the book is almost exactly as Jessie recounted it, with a few minor changes, to clarify some of the details or make it easier to read. It is mainly in chronological order but not entirely.

Janice Claxton

Foreword by Heather Phillips, Jessie's Daughter

This book has been written as part of the celebrations to mark my 90th birthday.

Having lived at Blackheath farm until I was ten, I spent a lot of time with my grandparents Jane and Robert, and all their visitors. They had much influence on my early years and my whole outlook on life, for which I am most grateful. I realise how lucky I was to have been brought up in such a happy and resourceful family. I had very few toys (only homemade ones) or books. My father took us out for walks on Sundays and helped me to appreciate all the footpaths, wild flowers, and birds in Wenhaston. Now I feel my early years were very privileged. All my family was hard working and self sustaining.

Acknowledgements
I would like to express my appreciation to Janice and Roger Claxton, who have made this book possible. I am very grateful for all the time and trouble they have taken to get my mother's story into print. Derek Newby gave us invaluable help and his expertise was much appreciated.
Joe Crowfoot, artist, kindly allowed us to include photos of three of his paintings.

Most of the photos were from my personal collection, and several were taken by my late husband, Peter. Some of them can be seen on the Wenhaston Archive, now hosted by the Southwold Railway Trust.

Proceeds from the sale of the book will be donated to Wenhaston Village Hall.

About the Appendix

This contains explanations of words and phrases used by Jessie, and some additional information.

How We Worked, Lived And Played, My Earliest Memories in the Cottage

I was born on 18th December 1896, in Wenhaston, Suffolk, in a sweet little cottage on the edge of common land covered with beautiful heather and gorse.

The house where Jessie was born

My Dad was a farm labourer, and when he made a full week his wage was only ten shillings, old money, he had to lose all wet days. My mum was a dressmaker.

We had a very large garden and grew lots of fruit and vegetables. We kept pigs and chickens, and had a horse and cart. My Mum drove to Lowestoft 16 miles away, which took 2 hours, and she sold them around the town so as to earn more money.

Jessie's mother, Jane Roberts aged 18. She made all her own clothes.

Jessie's father, Robert "Snotcher" Roberts in his fifties. The bottle contains cold tea.

The first thing I can remember was when I was ill with measles, and when I got better I sat in my high chair at the table. My brother, who was fourteen months older than me, went with a friend to gather me some primroses. When he came home he spread them all out on the table saying, "You don't know where I had to go to get them." His poor little hands were all scratched and bleeding. I can remember whispering to him, "Did you cry?"

I went to school when I was 3¼. My brother was 4½, so we started together. The following Xmas I was rewarded with a beautiful book for good conduct and proficiency, which I treasure very much, and I am keeping as a family heirloom. We also got a money prize at Xmas, for good attendance.

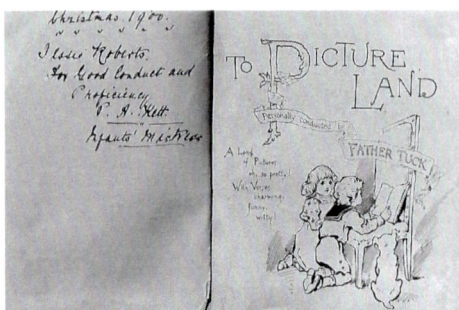

Jessie's book prize with inscription

The centre "pull out" from the book, with three dimensional pictures.

My brother and I got one almost every year as we were rarely away. If we had a cold or temperature, Mum would dissolve a piece of saltpetre in boiling water for us to drink. That was to get the temperature down, and during May we would be given a teaspoon of treacle and sulphur to purify our blood. That was Mum's remedy, and I never remember having a doctor all my school life, we were always fit and well.

Wenhaston School, as it was when Jessie attended. It had fine gates, a bell tower and chimneys then.

When we went to school we played hop-scotch, marbles and bowled our hoops. The girls had skipping ropes and skipped to school. We also spun our tops. We could do all this on the roads, as there was very little traffic. The young boys and girls can't do that today, the cars and lorries are terrible, even in our village. I'm so thankful we live on Blackheath; no wonder people retire to our lovely village, as I am writing I can hear the nightingale singing its lovely song.

When we were at school the boys made whistles and pop guns from elder wood; they loaded the pop guns with acorns, squeezed them into the barrel using the school wall. When the headmaster saw the state of the wall he was furious. He forbad all pop guns to be brought into the playground.

The Primitive Methodist Chapel

Almost on our doorstep was the Primitive Methodist Chapel, where we were sent to Sunday School morning and afternoon, and then to evening service. Most Sundays we had local preachers. One lady was called Mrs. Cordle, I remember her text so well. It was taken from Joshua "As for me and my house, we will serve the Lord".....Whenever she got held up for words she repeated the text. We got so amused and counted the times it was repeated. I've often thought since, what courage she had to preach so long to an almost full house.

I had an uncle whose name was Harry Self, he was partly crippled with frostbite when young. One Sunday a Mr. Holmes preached, he was very slow and boring, his text was about selfishness. After a long pause he shouted, is there a Mr. Self in this house. Poor old Harry, who always sat at the back of the chapel, near the tortoise stove which was very cosy, scratched his curly head. Most of the congregation turned and looked at Harry.

One Sunday I went to his house, he was reading the plan and said he was looking to see if old Holmes was preaching. "If so I ain't going." It just shows how careful and tactful one has to be when preaching from the pulpit.

In the early summer, we had a camp meeting, a lot of the forms were taken from the Chapel and put near the Black Deek, which was covered with a lovely small flower yellow and white, we called it egg and bacon, around the pond was maidenhair grass and oxeye daisies and the scent from the gorse was lovely.

My dad took his waggon onto the commons for the service to be conducted from. We had lovely Sankey hymns "Shall we gather at the river", "All things bright and beautiful", "Count your many blessings", "Blessed assurance, Jesus is mine", "The Glory song", and Wesley's lovely hymn "How can it be" which was a great favourite and "What a friend we have in Jesus".

The Primitive Methodist chapel on Blackheath. The oval date name plate on the front over the porch was removed when the chapel was sold to become a private residence.

My friend Elsie Freeman and I when I was older shared playing the organ and Elsie's friend Maud (Mona) Aldridge when staying at "Hill House" and helped with the singing. She had a very sweet voice. Mona's Dad lived and farmed at Brampton Hall and every August while he was there the Primitive Methodist conference was held, that was a great day. Mona was the mother of David Frost.

When I was 10 years old I signed the Pledge. A very nice family hired Red House Farm, Hinton. Their name was Pipe, he was an ex police officer. He had two grown up sons and daughter, they all became members of our chapel. Mr. Pipe formed the Band of Hope and most of the Sunday School children joined. We had very lively meetings. Mr. Pipe played the concertina and sang solos, one was called "On his ragged coat he wore a little bow of blue". His sons married and hired the Laurel Farm Wenhaston. After many years, farming was so bad they couldn't carry on, the farms were sold, and the oldest son and his family emigrated to Canada and all had to leave our Chapel, they were all missed very much.

For our Sunday School treat in the summer, we went to Dunwich in a waggon. My Dad lent his waggon and horses and bent elm branches over the top. We decorated it with flowers. It looked lovely. The church and Wesleyan Sunday School also went to Dunwich in waggons, it was a great day.

My step grandfather whose name was James Spoore was a member of the Wesleyan Chapel and when he was farming he lent his waggon and horses to take the children to Dunwich. One could pay if anyone else would like to go. One year some fishermen were home and as Harry Self was the horseman to my step grandfather he drove the waggon and horses, his was the last waggon.

After lunch these fishermen took Harry to the 'Ship' and treated him, Harry got rather merry. On the return home, they teased him about being the last to leave. The fishermen urged him to pass the other waggons. At the first opportunity to pass, Harry whipped his horses and galloped passed the others all singing and waving.

After Harry got home my step grandfather gave him such a lecture for bad behaviour. Poor old Harry had to go to the Wesleyan Chapel, go on the carpet and apologise, he was a fine character, I don't know if it was ever recorded. I think I have told you all I can remember of the happy days I spent at the Primitive Methodist Chapel.

Life On Blackheath, Criminal Events And Accidents

One part of Wenhaston was called Blackheath. My parents told me it got the name from all the fires lit on Guy Fawkes Day. It looked awful afterwards, all black and dirty, but when the new growth came it was lovely, the young gorse looked beautiful when in bloom. There was a lovely pond on the heath called 'Black Deek.' My parents thought it was a 'Dew Pond' as it was always full of water. In winter after a very hard frost we had lovely slides on the pond, and all the Wenhaston children came and enjoyed themselves. We on Blackheath felt a community of our own, and regarded the rest of the village as foreigners.

The dew pond (Black Deek) on Blackheath.
The cottage where Jessie was born is on the right.

In 1902 there was a terrible murder on the night of 31st May/1st June. The victim was a Rose Harsent, a strong young woman of 22 years, who was in service in a large house in Peasenhall, called Providence House. She was a member of Sibton P.M. Chapel. The accused was a married man with a family. William Gardiner was also a member of Sibton P.M. Chapel, an office bearer, Sunday School Superintendant, and a man held in high respect.

My mother went to a neighbour's house every night to read the newspaper, and follow the progress of the trial. There was a re-trial and Gardiner was found not guilty. My mum was very surprised at the verdict.

Postcards from the time, showing the house where Rose worked, and Mr. Gardiner's cottage.

There was a very bad thunderstorm on the night of the murder, and for many years about the same time as Rose Harsent was murdered, there was a very bad thunderstorm, which reminded us of the terrible murder.

My mum did so much dressmaking. She had her treadle sewing machine under the sitting room window, and she saw a lot of what was going on. Our neighbour's son, whose name was Fred Canham, worked at Hinton Hall. Another young man who lived in the village was named Toll Mayhew and also worked at Hinton Hall. Their boss gave them hedges to cut in winter in their spare time, and they kept the wood. When the boss went to Halesworth Cattle Sale every other Wednesday, he let these two young men have a horse and tumbrel to bring their wood home, this was done on every Sale Day. My mum saw them arrive with a load of wood, and a sack was taken out which looked as if it was corn, and another which looked like cattle beet, and then half the wood was unloaded and the other half was taken down the village to Mayhew's. This went on every Sale Day.

One Wednesday, Mum said there were three sacks taken out, one looked as if there was something alive in it as it squiggled about. Half of the wood was unloaded and the other half taken to Mayhew's, this went on until all the wood was brought home.

One day, our neighbour invited my Dad to look around his garden which he was very proud of, and Dad saw a small pig in the sty. Mum wondered if that was what she had seen squiggling about in the sack. Mum was so amused and told Dad all she had seen, but didn't say anything to anyone else, as she said what she saw was nothing to do with her. She always arranged her stitching on a Sale Day as she guessed what was going on.

When I was six years old my Dad hired Blackheath Farm, only 56 acres. Our cottage garden joined the farm meadow, so we didn't have far to move. My dad made a gate at the end of our garden which joined the meadow, so we could get to the farm easily, as my Grandmother lived at the farmhouse.

Blackheath Farm House, where Jessie grew up. The well, which was used for drinking water, is in the foreground.

My Dad had saved five lovely cockerels to give to his friends who had helped him, as Xmas presents. He fed them on the meadows every morning and afternoon, and at night time they would go back to the cottage to roost.

My Mum was very clever, no one could pull the wool over her eyes. One morning Dad came in and said "My cockerels are all gone, someone has stolen them." Mum told Dad, "Fred Canham has stolen them, and Toll Mayhew has received them," and she told Dad to go and report it to the police.

My Dad was very reluctant to report his neighbour, but Mum insisted and said "It's going to be nipped in the bud, if they'll take your only five cockerels, how many will they take when we rear a lot?" Dad went and reported it to the police, and told him what he thought. Dad said "I'll go and look in Toll's fowl house bye and bye." The policeman said

"Bugger bye and bye, you go now and if you see your cockerels don't leave them. I'll be in the blacksmith's shop which joins Mayhew's garden and if you don't come back, I'll come down." Dad didn't come back. He said "There are my cockerels." "Are you sure?" asked the policeman. "I'm certain," said Dad.

By this time the two men had left Hinton Hall, and were working at Laurel Farm, Wenhaston. I don't know if the boss at Hinton Hall smelt a rat and gave them the sack, or if they left on their own accord. The police told my Dad not to leave the fowl house, and he would go and fetch the two men. He went to Mayhew and accused him of receiving Snotcher's cockerels. (That was my dad's nickname). Mayhew denied hard and fast, they were not Snotcher's cockerels. When Canham saw the police had got Mayhew he was so upset he had to go behind a hay stack and relieve himself. After that the policeman told Canham about the cockerels, and he denied it, saying that they were not Snotcher's, they were Mayhew's. The policeman marched them down to the fowl house, still denying, they were not Snotcher's. He said "Catch the cockerels, put them in a crate and take them to Blackheath Farm. Let them out on the meadow, feed them and wait. When it begins to get dusk, see where they roost."

The cockerels started marching one behind the other, each in turn flew over the gate, marched up the garden path and straight to the fowl house where they were roosting happily, it was 'Home Sweet Home'. Then they both owned up. Canham said "I stole them and Mayhew received them." The next day both men were issued with a summons to appear at Saxmundham Magistrate Court on a certain day. I don't know how they got there as it was eleven miles from Wenhaston and no transport.

My Dad took the policeman and the cockerels in his horse and cart. The cockerels were taken into Court, both men pleaded guilty and were fined. They had to pay my Dad's day's work and expenses. My Dad said the men could ride home with him sitting on the crate. The police were furious and said "Let the buggers walk." My Dad didn't bear any malice or bitterness, and was always friends after. All the farmers around couldn't understand how Snotcher found out so quickly who stole his cockerels. They had been losing fowls for years and had no idea who stole them. My Mum said what they did and what she saw was nothing to do with her, but when they stole from my Dad that was a different story. No fowls were stolen for a very long time, so the thieving went on in the good old days, as they call them.

*Jessie with her brother James in 1908.
She was 11 or 12 and James was about a year older.*

I have had a very charmed life, being near to death on four occasions. In the first year my dad grew field peas, and after it was harvested lots of peas were left on the stubble, so he took a sow and a litter of pigs to clean it up. I was only 6½ and my brother 7¾ years old. He was with a teenage boy looking after the pigs. My Mum had been very busy making me a pretty dress out of one of her old ones. I remember it had a hanging pocket with a ribbon so I wanted to put it on. Mum and Dad were going to the field to see how the boys were getting on as it was bordered by common land and difficult to keep the pigs from getting onto the common. I wanted to stay with the boys. Mum and Dad had gone home, and as I was going to join them they shouted to me to go and stop the pigs from going on the common.

I ran after the pigs, the sow ran after me, caught me and mauled me for 12 yards and tore all my pretty dress to pieces. I was bruised and had teeth marks all over my body, and then it started eating my arm. The boys rushed to me and whipped the sow until I could get away. My brother tried to lead me home, a neighbour heard me crying, rushed out and picked me up and carried me home.

I was in a dreadful state with blood and shock. I had the most dreadful arm and the nearest doctor lived in Halesworth, about four miles away. My Dad hurried and put the horse in the cart to take me to the Doctor's. My Grandmother *(Granny Spoore)* who lived in part of the farmhouse, rushed out to look at my arm. I remember her saying "You can take that horse out of the cart, I can get that arm well."

She was a wonderful nurse, and had healed many wounds. My arm was eaten to the bone, luckily the bone wasn't damaged, the boys were there just in time. My Grandmother went into the garden and gathered a bunch of parsley, washed and cut it up, scalded some bread with boiling water, grated pure brown soap, and pure brown sugar and made a lovely poultice. She cleaned the wound and how the poultice soothed it, it was so soft and warm. It was repeated twice a day. For years how I loved the smell of parsley, and remembered how it helped to heal my wound.

While this was happening to me, my cousin was in service in London with two ladies who had a holiday home in Walberswick. Their names were Buncombe. They wrote to my Mum and said they would like to see me and would Mum meet a certain train at Wenhaston, on the Southwold Railway. When the train came in they were standing by the door. We were there, they shook hands with Mum and kissed me and said how sorry they were such a thing could happen to such a small child. As the train was leaving they handed a large box to my Mum as my arm was in a sling.

17

I was very anxious wondering what was in the box, and when Mum unpacked it there was a most beautiful doll, the first and only one I ever had, which gave me hours of pleasure.

On the following Saturday my Mum had to go to Lowestoft with a load of fruit and vegetables etc. My mum took Sarah who was a friend, to look after me. The horse was put in a stable at a pub called 'The Stone Cottage'. There was a plain outside where one could stand. After Mum had given the horse a lovely bait, she took a large basket of green peas to a greengrocer's shop over the road. I ran away from Sarah, I was so quick and rushed after my Mum. I was knocked down by a large fish dray with four wheels, and two horses. I was under the wheel. Luckily the driver pulled up in time to stop me from being crushed to death, my head was badly cut.

I was picked up and rushed to the chemist's shop nearby. I remember the chemist shouting "Go away, no one is killed," as a large crowd had gathered around the shop. The chemist dressed the wound in my head and bandaged it up. Luckily it did not damage my arm as it was well padded. I was given a lovely box of sweets and was very happy and grateful when I came out.

Sarah

My poor Mum was so distressed and said "Sarah, why did you let her go?" Poor Sarah, who was such a kindly soul said "If that child had been killed I would have been blamed." Of course it was my fault, I should never have run away from Sarah, that was my second life saved.

18

The Gypsy Family On Blackheath

When we lived at the cottage, some of our neighbours were gypsies: four sisters and a brother – Rana, Lovie, Nelly and Sally, and the brother was Lomas. Their surname was Pickett. They took a piece of land from the common and built a very large tent, they all lived and slept in it. They had a round stove, I think it was called a 'Tortoise'. The tent was always warm and comfortable. The floor was covered with piece rugs made from old clothes, they all sat on the floor with legs crossed.

They were all very industrious. All the girls had large hampers filled with all sorts of things such as tape, lace, ribbon, needles and pins, cotton thread etc. They each had their own route, different ones each day. They travelled miles. The brother stayed at home making pegs from wood from the hedges, grinding scissors and making lanterns; he was always busy. The girls made 'dock ointment' which they sold, it was supposed to be very good, they would never give the recipe away, so it died with them.

The Pickett family. Rana, Lovie, Sally, Nelly, their brother Lomas with their mother.

After a time a Gypsy Evangelist pitched a tent on the common. He was ordered off, so he hired a field from my Dad. A huge tent was put on the field filled with chairs and an organ. There was a large family of fine looking boys and the daughter played the organ, their name was Boswell. As they were gypsies the Picketts went to all the services, the tent was full of people and the singing was lovely. Their favourite hymn seemed to be 'When I survey the wondrous cross", it sounded so lovely as everyone seemed to know it so well.

The Picketts were so impressed, none of them could read or write, and as the Bible was read to them all were converted and became Christians, and led a very good life. Mind you, they were never any trouble and were greatly respected. Ever after, they went to the Wesleyan Chapel twice on Sundays, and were very religious.
One day when my Dad came home from the fields he saw a Rolls Royce car outside the gypsies. Lomas came to the farm every morning for the milk; he said a friend had visited him the day before. Lomas said "I saved him from the foot and mouth disease." He added that he had fed him when he was destitute and given him boots so he could carry on. After that the man worked very hard, got a lot of money together, and was able to buy a greengrocer's business in Yarmouth. After a time he became Mayor of Yarmouth. I'm not sure, but I think Lomas said his name was 'Rawlings'.

He never forgot the gypsies and brought them large quantities of fruit and vegetables. One day when Dad came home he said "Just look over the common." We rushed down the drift – coming over the common was a steam engine puffing along, a cloud of smoke pouring from the chimney, dragging a railway carriage which was taken to the gypsies' site. The girls made very nice bedrooms in the carriage, they had one each. It was so interesting, I expect they thought they lived their lives like other people. They were never short of visitors, and children from the Sunday School went and read the Bible to them. Sally, the youngest sister, was tall dark and handsome. She told my mother she had an offer of marriage from a very rich man, but she refused as she preferred to live her gypsy life with her brother and sisters.

Stella, and Hard Work On The Farm

When I went to school we had a bully, she was clever and always top of the class. Most of the girls treated her as a queen. I did not have much to do with her as she was so domineering. One day she got wrong with a very nice girl called Stella. Poor Stella stood against the school wall; they all marched past and jeered her. I wanted to befriend Stella, but I was too frightened I would be treated the same way. Stella went home and cried, and didn't want to go to school the next day, and her Mum wanted to know why. She was Scottish and wasn't afraid to say what she thought. She went to school the next morning and saw the headmaster. She told him how Stella had been treated and he was furious. Didn't he give the school a lecture first thing in the morning, and said he would march them around the playground until they were all friends. It never happened again. After that Stella and I were very great friends, until the end of her life.

After we left school we often went for lovely walks, as we were both fond of nature, and studied wild flowers. Poor Stella was stricken with an illness, I never knew what it was. When my Mum went to Lowestoft she bought a lovely piece of fish for me to take to Stella. She died very young, and the hymn which was chosen for her funeral was "Oh for a closer walk with God", and when the second verse was sung I was so grieved, I just broke down:

What peaceful hours we once enjoyed,
How sweet the memories still;
But they have left an aching void
The world can never fill.

I could never understand why Stella was treated in this way. I often wonder if it was jealousy as her Dad had a wheelwright business, and they lived in a very nice house. All my life I have experienced how cruel jealousy can be.

As the years went by we all had to work very hard. I always had to go home straight from school and do lots of jobs, as Mum was always dressmaking.

My brother, who was clever took an exam and left school at 13 years, otherwise he would have had to go until he was 14 years old. He worked on the farm and did a man's job, going to plough with two horses. He stayed on the farm for three years.

As all the young lads when they left school went fishing, from Lowestoft on drifters (which was the home fishing), most of them came home with lots of money. My brother got dissatisfied in working for very little money, and couldn't see any prospects in farming, so he got a berth with my Uncle Jack, as cook on 'The Colonial'. My Mum taught him to make light dumplings etc. and made him slops with grey calico, dyed them brown with 'cutch' (which they used to preserve the nets). Cutch was made from the barks of trees.

Lowestoft fishermen in slops. This photo is from 1906.

He went fishing from September to Xmas, and when he came home he had six golden sovereigns. He had a few weeks at home then went mackerel fishing, I think it was around Cornwall and Ireland. He came home in the Spring, and after that went herring fishing around Scotland, and later on came home fishing from Lowestoft. In those days fishing was a good industry. The harbour was full of drifters, many from Scotland. The Scottish girls came and gutted the herrings for kippers. It was wonderful to see them working and doing the job so quickly.

I left school at 14 years in 1910, and stayed at home with my parents working very hard. My maternal grandmother was a widow and lived in a small cottage. The first thing every morning I went and lit her fire, gave her breakfast, cleaned up the bed-sitting room, and helped to dress her. This went on from December until harvest, when it was decided she should give up her cottage, and have a bed-sitting room at the farm. This meant I could do more in the mornings on the farm. In the spring, before the corn was planted, I went stone picking. I had an apron made from a sack, and picked the stones into the apron, then emptied it into a pail which held a peck.

I had to fill the pail thirty six times for a load. It took three pails for a bushel, and twelve bushels for a load. I managed to pick a load by 12 o'clock dinner time.

I did the same in the afternoon, and left off after I had picked another load altogether seventy two pails. I put a stone in a row every time I emptied the pail so I didn't make a mistake. I got very tired. In those days these stones were used to repair the roads. Sarah lived in a cottage on my way home, she was so kind and thoughtful, and told me to call in after I had finished. She would make me a lovely cup of cocoa, and she always had a very nice caraway seed cake, didn't I enjoy it.

I was so willing to work hard and help my parents, as I knew how hard it was to get a living by farming in those days. I was well kept, we always had good wholesome food.

Mum always clothed me well as she made most of my clothes. I was always taken to Whist Drives, which was one of the joys of my life. I was never paid any money, it was a labour of love.

Jessie at the farm with her parents Jane and Robert Roberts. Jessie is on the right. Anna Mayhew (born Self) is in the middle at the back and her daughter Maggie in front on the right.
Anna's mother Mary Ann Self died young in childbirth, so Jane helped to bring Anna up.

The First World War

The First World War broke out in 1914, I never joined the Land Army, so I didn't have a uniform, but I was registered and issued with an armlet and a certificate as I was at home helping my Dad all I could.

Jessie's certificate for working in agriculture during the first World War

He went to plough all day, cleaned and cut the mangel worzels with the machine, ready for the horses after a hard day's work. Before they went into the stable, they were taken to the Black Deek for water, and then I would go and fetch the cows home from the marshes for milking. After all the jobs were done outside, I would go indoors and prepare the tea, as Mum would be busy sewing.

After Spring, came hay-making. When it was ready, Dad would cut the grass into rows to dry with a scythe. Mum and I would rake it into large heaps ready to be put on the waggon, and stacked to mature for the horses in the winter. After haysel came harvest. My dad and his mate would cut the corn with a scythe, and after a hot day or two we would gavel it into large heaps. This would be barley ready to be carted and put on a stack.

The wheat was scythed and tied up into sheaves, and then we had to put ten sheaves together to make a shock, so it stood up on its own, until ready to be carted and stacked.

As we had a large house we had soldiers billeted on us. They had two double beds in each room. We had eight soldiers. After the first night, before we made the bed, two officers called and asked if we had any complaints. My Mum said they were all well behaved and very nice young men.

When we went to make the beds I was very anxious, and was looking to see anything alive, such as fleas or lice. My Mum wanted to get the beds made, and wanted to know what I was looking for. When I said what I thought she said they didn't have such things in this country. All at once I saw a body lice, and then we got worried. We put it in a matchbox and hunted all the beds and blankets all morning, but didn't find any more so we had to report it. Mum said "That's why the officers came."

We were told afterwards that the regiment was noted for that. The soldiers who slept in the bed had to go to Beccles to be fumigated, and we had two fresh soldiers, and had no more trouble. They didn't want to leave the farm staying several weeks, and were then sent abroad.

Lowestoft was getting bombed and we had evacuees from Kessingland for a few weeks, we were always kept busy.

Postcard showing the bombing in Lowestoft in 1916

My brother's boat was taken over by the Government. By that time my brother had passed his 'Mates' certificate, and was second in command. My favourite Uncle Jack was in command, and they were sent to the Dardanelles during the war, mine sweeping. They came home safely, but the strain was too much for my Uncle. My brother had to bring the boat home. They had a rough journey through the Bay of Biscay, the engineer asked "Are you driving us to Hell?" They had to call at Lisbon to be made sea worthy and were only allowed 24 hours. They landed in Falmouth, Cornwall in 1918.

My uncle was taken into hospital, and died there. He was given a military funeral in Wenhaston.

He was such a good man and I admired him so much, I always said if I married and had a son, he should be called Jack Roberts. If he was only half as good a man as my Uncle I would be very happy. After I married I had a son, and he has been well worthy of his name, as you can hear later in my story.

My uncle Jack (Harry) Roberts
In his Naval uniform.

LOWESTOFT STEAM DRIFTER "COLONIAL"
from an original painting by, Joe Crowfoot
copyright, joecrowfootartist@yahoo.co.uk

Jack's boat, a steam drifter based in Lowestoft

During the First World War we wanted to raise money for a peace celebration fund. My dearest friend was Elsie Freeman. We shared playing organ at the Primitive Methodist Chapel. I often went to their home at Hill House where we had lovely times. Her parents entertained the soldiers who were billeted at Bulcamp Workhouse, as it was then called. Mrs. Freeman was a Guardian of the Workhouse. It is now called Blythburgh Hospital. It is much different now, but the stigma still stays with my generation. My opinion is that it should have been used for more business purposes, and to give work to all the boys when they came home, instead of being thrown on the dole. The cost of making it into a hospital must have been enormous. Another hospital should have been built in the district with all that money, which would have found work for our builders who couldn't afford to carry on.

We raised money by having concerts. I had been very busy all day taking up carrots on the farm, and had to use a fork as they were very

A governess cart

hard to get out of the ground. I stabbed my ankle with the fork, got home, washed and changed my clothes and had tea. I then went to Hill House to practise for a play. I walked down to Hill House quite alright, my ankle felt sore but I could walk alright. After sitting all the evening reading through the play, I couldn't walk, my foot had got so stiff. Elsie got the pony and governess cart out, and drove me home.

Her family were all such kind people. When we had a concert they wanted a boy and girl to sing "If you were the only boy in the world and I was the only girl". As I had rather a strong voice, I was asked if I would be the girl. Only one boy volunteered, and that was a boy I couldn't stand. He rather pestered me and was only too pleased to join in the song. You can imagine how I felt, I had to forget all about that.

It was the only act to get an encore, so I couldn't have done it so badly, but it would have been much nicer if it had been someone I really liked.

During the war Zeppelins were coming over. When we heard them, we all got up. We saw from our bedroom window one brought down at Theberton, it was all in flames. As we were watching, pieces of black fabric floated past our window, it was all very worrying. Some airmen were killed and buried in the churchyard. After many years, in 1960, they were taken up and moved to the German Cemetery in Cannock Chase.

Zeppelin 48, which came down over a field in Theberton on 16th June 1917. It was taking part in an attempted air raid over London.

LOCAL ATTRACTION: Crowds of curiosity seekers arrive to take a look at the downed zeppelin at Theberton in 1917

Photograph G. MCKERROW

Farming, Visitors and Evacuees

After the war, farming was very bad, especially in the early twenties. I persuaded my Mum to take in visitors. We let most of our bedrooms, parlour and dining room. We charged one guinea a room per week, and 7/6 for attendance, we were very soon booked up. Mr. Scrimgeor from Blyford Hall came and viewed the rooms. He had been to many farm houses, but he thought Blackheath Farm house was the best and cleanest he had seen.

He booked them for five weeks for Major Firth, his wife, five children and a nurse. I think Mr. Scrimgeor was a Captain in Major Firth's regiment. They brought all their own food in, and my Mum cooked and made them beautiful meals. They came every year as they were so happy. We were full up until the end of September.

It was very hard going in those days, no bathroom, no water laid on and no sewage. We had to fetch the water from the well, which was 65ft deep. I had to fill some ewers with cold water, and take large enamel jugs of hot water for each bedroom, every morning.

The toilet was outside covered with ivy; it was a double seater, one for adults and one for children, and a pail which my Dad emptied early every morning then lime washed it out. We had no toilet paper in those days. I cut newspaper into nice squares and hung them on the door every morning. As it was covered in ivy, I painted on the door 'Ivy Cottage'. Dad built one for ourselves, so the visitors had their own.

I have often been asked, which of the visitors we had at the farm did I like the best – I answered that I liked them all, but the most interesting was the Firth family. Major Firth's wife was Dorothy, and the children were John 2 years, Tony 4 years, Barbara 6 years, Joan 8 years and Richard 11 years old.

Three of the Firth children, probably John, Tony and Barbara.

They came from Bedford, and liked to take the children to Southwold when the weather was suitable. Joan didn't get on very well with the rest of the family, and often Mrs. Firth would ask if Joan could stay with me. I was always pleased to have her. Joan was very advanced and clever. I often said to Mum "I wonder what will happen to Joan when she grows up?" – she was so happy with me and would say "Jessie, may I scrub the door steps?" I'd say "Yes, if you put your apron on, so you don't dirty your pretty dress." She wanted to polish the cutlery.

We had a young lad working on the farm, she would say "Can I go and have a chat with Cyril?" and I'd say she could if she didn't stay long. She was a very obedient child, and would have lunch with us in the kitchen and was so happy. After lunch she would help me to lay the table ready for when her family came home. After all the jobs were done we would go to the common and gather wild flowers. She knew the names of most of them, and I would tell her those she didn't know. I would give her a vase for the flowers, and she arranged them for the table.

Mr. Scrimgeor lived at Blyford Hall, but his parents lived at Wissett Hall, and invited the Firth family over to meet them. Tony was dressed so prettily, he came into the kitchen and said "Look at the nice boy already for the party," - he was only 4 years old. They all went to Wissett Hall, the children were put upstairs in the nursery with their nurse, and no other children, and all the elders were downstairs. Tony got so bored, he got away from the nurse and went downstairs, straight to the hostess saying, "You call this a party? We're put in the nursery and you're down here having all the nice things." Dorothy said, "I tried to push him behind me but he wouldn't stop and kept saying Horrid Party." When they came home Dorothy said, "Tony disgraced us, of course I should not have told him it was a party."

One morning, the Major and Dorothy were walking around the lawn so lovingly, when they came into the kitchen and Dorothy was crying. Mum said "Why are you so sad?" The Scrimgeors of Blyford Hall were giving them a farewell dance but Dorothy told us that she couldn't possibly go as she had damaged her pretty green silk dress and stockings at the last dance. Mum said "Bring them to me, and I will see if I can repair them." I said I would prepare the evening meal. Mum was all afternoon repairing and pressing, so the repair was hardly noticeable. When they came home they came into the kitchen, the Major said "Dorothy was the belle of the ball, and all through your kindness."

They stayed five weeks and some time after they returned home, near to Christmas all the children went to a party. Dorothy wrote and told me how Joan came home, dancing full of joy. They all went to bed and Joan was awakened with a very bad pain. It grew worse and worse. At last the doctor got her into hospital She has a burst gland and was full of poison. She died on Christmas Day. When I got the letter, I was so grieved and wept all day. Had she been my own child I couldn't have felt it more.

I went out and bought some flowers, and made a wreath. I packed it off as soon as possible. Afterwards I had a letter from Dorothy. I still have that letter, and all my life I have never forgotten that child.

She was laid to rest out in a sweet county Church yard near Bedford - a place she loved - under a small oak tree near the beautiful Tower of Elstow Church. She who loved the county So. on the sudden terrible anguish shock

Page six of the original letter, which was kept by Jessie.

Jan 9th 1921

My dear Jessie,

Your sweet wreath arrived so fresh and beautiful. Major Firth and I treasured it more than all the others. It was just <u>made</u> by you with all your love and sympathy and all the sweet memories of Joan.

I <u>can't</u> realise she isn't here with all her laughing gay ways and her dear naughtiness and her love and sweetness. You knew and understood her so <u>perfectly</u> and she loved you so – in fact all of you and often said "Oh! I wish I was back with Jessie and the ducks. I <u>loved</u> the farm."

Just four and a half days of ghastly illness. She and Barbara were <u>perfectly</u> well on the Thursday. Both went to a party and came dancing home full of joy at 7 o'clock. She slept all night and wakened at 6 with a cry of pain in stomach. She grew worse all day – the doctor came again and again and at last at 11 0'clock that night they took her to the Nursing Home and operated. She nearly died then. They found a gland had burst in her stomach containing this awful poison. She lived all Sat: and Sunday and on Monday there was great hope – but as they wore on the poison spread upwards first to the lungs and then Oh! Jessie to the brain – I can't tell you the agony of the Xmas Eve, to watch that darling child – Xmas Day came and all hope was gone. She gradually sank into unconsciousness and passed peacefully away at 9.15 on Xmas Night. She was laid to rest out in a sweet country church yard near Bedford, a place she loved – under a sweet oak tree near the beautiful Tower of Elstow Church. She loved the country so. Oh! The sudden terribly anguished shock of it all.

Jessie, we must just think of her joy and her peace – perhaps God felt her life might be very hard and difficult with her beautiful face and her highly strung nervous temperament. He knows for us the sorrow of loss and a gap in our sweet family and that can never be replaced. But she is just ours forever in her sweet bright youth never to grow old or to grow away. Joan with all her love and deep affection – always so tender to all living things, so loving in her joy of flowers and country. Major Firth is heartbroken. How he loved her. I long to see you and talk of her to you. Goodbye dear Jessie, I know how you all loved her and she you. With our love and Barbara sends you a kiss. I will send you a photo of her but we had no good one – only snap shots. We are staying away for a week's rest and return on Tuesday next,

    Yours ever sincerely
    Dorothy E. Firth

We took the wreath out ourselves and it looked so sweet and fresh. Thank you so much and dear Mrs. Roberts and all of you.
Her birthday was Monday last Jan 7th. She would have been 8 years old.

She was buried under the beautiful tower of Elstow Church, under a lovely oak tree. After my husband retired we went on holiday with some friends, and went through Bedford. I said I would like to see Elstow Church. When we got there we went into the church, and then I looked for Joan's grave. There, under this lovely oak tree was Joan's little gravestone, so well maintained. I just stood and wept.

Years went by, and Major Firth retired. He did so much good work, and joined so many organisations, he was such a kind man. He died in similar circumstances to Joan. Dorothy sent me the newspaper with his funeral, and the reports of the good he had done in his life time. There was almost a whole page. It told how in all his life he didn't even pass a tramp on the road without giving him a lift. I have never forgotten that family.

*Elstow Abbey Church, where Joan
Firth was buried*

During the First World War, a lady called to see if Mum could take her in for a few weeks. She was not happy where she was, and had four very young boys. As my parents were very fond of children they were pleased to have them. Her husband was away at the war. The children's names were James, Arthur, Tony and Jack. They were very happy and interested in the farm.

One afternoon Jack was missing, we didn't know where to look for him. We looked all around the pond, all over the common. All at once we saw him with the teenage boy who had gone to the marshes to fetch the cows for milking. He was coming along, like a little man with a stick, he was only three years old. When his Mum said "Jack, how could you go away from your mother?" He spoke very nicely, and although he had never been away from his mother before, his answer was "Well, I don't really want a mother much now." He was feeling very grown up. After the war they went back to their home, had a daughter and twins, a boy and a girl. Mr. and Mrs. Dodd bought a house in the village of

Wenhaston when they retired. We were always great friends, they were a very interesting family, all the children had good careers, and did very well.

One morning Mum received a letter from two maiden ladies who had been recommended to the farm for a holiday. We imagined they were elderly ladies as the letter was so precise. They came from Croydon, and were coming to Wenhaston on the Southwold Railway, Mum and I met them at the station with the horse and trap as it was a mile to the farm.

Southwold Railway near the Heronry
Painted by Joe Crowfoot, based on a photo taken by Jessie's
husband Goldie.
This was on the route the girls took to Southwold.
Copyright Joe Crowfoot.

When they got off the train we were so surprised. Mum said "They are two dear little girls!" One was 16 years old, and the other 18 years old. They said the train journey had been very interesting, and the scenery was beautiful. They very soon settled down, and had a good meal. Afterwards I went in their room and had a chat with them, and told them the interesting places they could visit.

The next day they went to Southwold, and were so impressed they were going again the next day, and on the Belle Steamer to Felixstowe. I told them if the sea got rough, the steamer wouldn't be able to stop at Southwold Pier, it would have to go on to Lowestoft. "If this should happen" I told them, "you would have to take a bus from Lowestoft to Wangford, send Mum a wire, and we will meet you at Wangford as it is 5 miles from Wenhaston." Well, this did happen – the horse was on the marshes. Her name was Jessie; Dad named her after me as she was such a little worker. She wasn't in the mind to be caught, we had a bit of a chase. At last she came to me, I grabbed her mane and Dad put a halter on and led her home.

We hurried to Wangford, the bus was just in and the girls were so grateful I had warned them. The girls came every year for their holiday. Beth the youngest, came and stayed a month at a time, lived and dined with us, and learned how to pluck and draw poultry. Beth was with us so much she became such a good friend, she was chief bridesmaid at my wedding, and Godmother to my daughter.

One day Mum wanted a rabbit for dinner, so Dad and Beth got the ferret in, he found he had forgotten to take a net. He took off his straw hat, held it over the hole. The rabbit came out of the hole at such a speed it went clean through the crown of his straw hat. How Beth laughed, she just couldn't stop. Dad said "I wonder what Mother will say, crown out of my hat, and no rabbit for dinner." Mum took everything as it came, and told him he'd find another hat in the attic, and that one would do for a scarecrow. After that they took a net and caught a lovely rabbit.

While Beth was staying with us in Wenhaston she met a very nice boy, got married, and had a very successful business in Croydon. Unfortunately she died in childbirth. Her sister Marjorie married and had a son. After he grew up and qualified as a doctor of medicine, he emigrated to Tasmania. After a time Marjorie went out there on holiday, and there she died. I was even a benefactor in her will, we were always great friends.

My maternal grandmother *(Granny Spoore)* who lived with us, was bedridden for five years, and in all that time she never had a bedsore. Mum and I blanket washed her every night, and gave her a nice rub with medicated spirit. I spent many hours with her in the evenings, as she had so many interesting stories to tell me. I wish I could remember them all. Her own mother died when she was only 21 years old. My Dad was called 'Snotcher' because his eldest sister had cut his ear while she was cutting his hair. She named him 'Snotcher' there and then and he carried this name to his grave.

As farming got worse many farmers went bankrupt. One day a large farmer who was also a dealer, came to see my Dad. When my Mum saw him talking to my Dad, she said "I would at least see the devil as see him, he already owes us for seed clover, he'll get something out of him." We had a very nice bullock which Dad was putting into the Xmas Sale. This farmer offered him £20; as Dad thought it would only make £15 in the sale, also transport expenses and the charge for selling, he sold it to this dealer. Mum was furious and said "You won't get your money." "Yes I will" said Dad who trusted everybody. After three weeks the farmer went bankrupt and Dad lost the bullock and the money.

Lots of farmers couldn't understand how Snotcher carried on. One farmer said his wife and daughter carried him, that was why I had no money, but was happy to do all I could to help my parents on the farm. I didn't want to see them turned out and nowhere to go.

After all the visitors had gone, I went blackberrying five days a week. I got up at dawn, walked to Hinton and nearly to Dunwich all alone; a girl wouldn't dare to do that today. The berries on Blackheath were picked by the local ladies, so if you wanted a good day's work, you had to get away on your own, picking clean as you go along. I took lots of bags called 'dorothy bags', made from rushes so they were easy to carry. I had a basket which held a 'peck' (12 lbs) to fill, and emptied it into the bags. When I had filled all the bags I hid them under a gorse bush, and covered them with bracken. My Mum would come along with the horse and cart and bring boxes to empty the bags in. By the end of the day I had often picked seven pecks, the most I ever picked was eight pecks one day, that was 96 lbs.

One day as I was on my way towards Dunwich, blackberrying, a Mr. Elmy was cutting bracken on Hinton Walks. He shouted to his mate who came from Wenhaston "If I was a young man I'd be looking around her, I never saw such a worker, she must be up at dawn the amount of berries she picks. I know it's right, she sometimes leaves them with my wife and her mother comes and picks her up with the horse and cart."

That day I felt very lonely and melancholy. We had such a hot dry summer, the poor farmer who lived at St. Helena Farm, Nr. Dunwich, had committed suicide. All his corn was scorched up on the sandy soil, and couldn't be harvested. I was so thankful when I heard our horse trotting along the road to pick me up. There are no blackberries around there now, it's all forestry.

One day I went blackberrying with my Mum, we wandered on to a laydown near Bramfield where we found some lovely berries. We hadn't been there long, when a short sturdy woman came and ordered us off. My Mum was a tall fine looking woman, and looked her up and down, before saying, "You're not very big but you're very bossy." The woman answered "I've been told that before." "And you're not ashamed to know it?" said my Mum. "Certainly not," she replied. My Mum said "People come on my farm and I don't order them off." My Mum told her if she didn't get up early and get them first, it was her fault as they were God's wild fruit and she thought they were free for all. As we were going away the woman shouted "Go to your own farm if you have one." All the years I went blackberrying that was the only time I was ordered off.

I went all around Sir Ralph Blois' estate. The game-keepers name was Muttitt, he lived in a cottage on Blythburgh Fenn. He knew my Mum quite well. He told her "Your daughter don't give me any trouble, she picks for hours both sides of a hedge. I saw her one day, hiding her berries under a gorse bush, covering them up with bracken to disguise them. I had a good mind to go and shift them, but had second thoughts." I had no idea I was being watched, otherwise I wouldn't have felt very comfortable.

I also went on Barnes estate – the gamekeeper's name was Shepherd. He lived in a cottage in Dingle, near Dunwich. He was very kind and told me where I could find some lovely berries. When we went picking near Blythburgh Lodge, I didn't like the gamekeeper very much. His name was Andrew List, a great big man who wore buskins made of leather to keep the bottom of his trousers dry. He nearly always carried a gun.

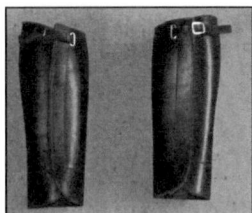

Buskins

He knew my mother very well, and often had a chat with her. He would say how my grandmother was the best woman he ever had in his house, when she nursed his wife at her confinement. He sort of frightened me somehow, he was so very loud I couldn't go there alone. Mum said he was alright, his bark was worse than his bite.

When I was young, farming was very bad from 1910 – 1925. I think that was the very worst time. My Dad grew beautiful malting barley. After it was threshed and dressed he took a sample to Halesworth Market. When he came home Mum asked him if he had sold it, and he told her he didn't get an offer. He bought some pigs, had the corn ground at Blythburgh Mill (as there was no help from the Government at that time). The buildings were in a bad state, the pig sties were wet and cold, so after a time the pigs got cramp and had great difficulty getting up. It took a long time to get them fit for market.

My Dad grew 'clog' wheat, it was planted in the autumn. After I had finished stone-picking, I had to go and pull docks out of the wheat before they seeded, put them on a heap and burn them. There were no weed killers in those days. My hands got sore and blistered, but still I carried on.

After the barley was planted and getting near harvest, a lot of corn 'cockle' came up, which all had to be pulled out as the barley and corn cockle seeds would not separate when dressed. Now with all the weed killers corn cockle is almost extinct. My son got me some seed and my daughter planted some in my garden where I can see it, to remind me of my youth.

Corn cockle flowers

When my Dad hired the farm he agreed to pay the 'tithes' – one was £20 and the other £10 a year, so that £30 was added to the rent, and it was called Queen Anne's Bounty. If you refused to pay it the State would come and take one tenth of your crop. A farmer who lived in Oulton Broad refused to pay the tithe. His name was Mobbs. He was dispossessed, his stock was sold. His friends bought it back for him so the tithe was paid and the farmer given what was left, that was the only way he would pay it. Sometime after, the tithe was abolished, every land owner had to pay a lump sum, so that was the end of Queen Anne's Bounty.

Family Life, Hard Work, Good Food

That was a very bad time, no wonder farmers couldn't carry on. My parents had no money behind them, no banking account at that time. It was hand to mouth, but we weathered the storm. One day my Dad took some pigs to the Sale. He went to the office and collected £15 and put it in his pocket, as he thought. When he got home the money wasn't there; whether he dropped it thinking he had put it in his pocket, or maybe someone watched him and stole it we never knew.

Mum did all the business, putting out a reward, but it was never returned. Mum took it all so calmly, she had a very brave and strong character. At that time £15 was a lot of money, today farmers are well off, with no tithe to pay, and a lot of help from the Government. They were helped to grow more than the government was able to sell, so with all the cost of storage for corn, butter and cheese, I feel they were helped too much, considering how farmers were treated in the twenties. I enjoy going around the country, to see beautiful farm houses and buildings restored. In earlier years the farm houses and buildings often looked a disgrace, so that has been money well spent.

My Mum took all our blackberries to Lowestoft, and bought all the others picked by other people, for which she paid a penny a pound, and sold them at 1½d per pound. She sold them all around the town, and during the home fishing, she would bring bags of fish home from Wenhaston fishermen for their families, and the men would give Mum lovely bags of fish for herself. My brother and I (when we were still at school) would go all around the village selling them at three a penny; sometimes we were very late, people waited up for us as they knew we would be around. We always finished up at Thorington Corner where a large family called Flatt lived. They would always take all we had left. All the rest of the fish Dad would put in salt, one night for bloaters, and two or three nights in salt for red herrings. For this my Dad made a smoke house; he lit a fire with oak wood and oak saw-dust. The next day we would have bloaters for tea, they were delicious.

When my Granny lived at the farm she baked in a brick oven. It was entirely bricked in, long, wide and oval shaped. It had to be heated with a faggot of wood until all the bricks were white hot. The bread would be all ready in the tins, the wood would burn the bricks clean in the oven, and the bread would be put inside with a tool called a 'peel'. Each loaf would be put on the peel, put to the end of the oven until it was full, then closed up with a steel door. As the oven cooled down the bread would be ready to come out.

My Granny sold bread to most of the people on the heath. When my Mum moved to the farm, she couldn't be bothered with the mess of the brick oven, so she had a 'Dutch' oven put in. It was a strong steel oven, with a grate underneath; when it got hot it baked lovely, you lit an ordinary fire with sticks and coal, it was much cleaner and easier.

When I was young we lived very differently to how we do today. For the winter Dad would have a pig killed, it would be all cut up, most of it would be put in the pot in salt. We had the pigs fry baked, and a piece of loin for roasting. After the pork had been in salt, Mum would get a nice piece of bread, soak it in water overnight and draw out some of the salt, cut it into small pieces with a good size onion chopped up finely, make a pork and onion dumpling. She would make a piece of pastry, roll a piece for the bottom, put on the pork and onion, a piece of pastry on top, nip them together, put them in a pudding cloth and boil for two hours.

When it was turned out of the cloth on to a dish and cut up, it would float in juice. The smell and the taste was delicious. We had cabbage, carrots and potatoes with it. The rest of the pork we would have cooked the next day hot with vegetables. What was left, we would have cold with mashed potatoes and pickled onion. It was simply lovely, and how it warmed our crops.

I remember that most of all I enjoyed it, after sliding on the pond. With the stock from the pork, Mum would make pea soup, by soaking the peas overnight, this would be delicious with all sorts of vegetables and light dumplings.

We always baked on Fridays for the week. That would include potato pie. Potato pie would be cooked with small pieces of pork and onion, and cooked potatoes put in a pie pan with a pastry crust on, that was very sustaining. We had lovely rabbit pie cold, there would be beautiful jelly. Wild rabbits were very tasty then, with no disease. We also had cold giblet pie, with all the giblets from the chickens. My Dad had his wheat ground so we always had plenty of whole meal flour.

Mum made butter and cheese, we had our own eggs, so we were almost self-supporting. Every week we had a joint of brisket from the butcher. We had gravy, Yorkshire pudding and vegetables, but no meat on Sundays. The gravy was so different then, and not a bit like it is today. On Monday we would have the meat cold with mashed potatoes and pickles. Brisket was a very sweet joint although it needs longer cooking; it was always on the bone.

When Dad killed a pig we had lots of fat. Mum fried that into lard, and then we had lovely scraps, which we had for tea with bread and butter. We had suet puddings, and the legs of pork would go in to pickle for a few days, then smoked in the storehouse with oak wood and sawdust, until they were ready to come out. They were then put into a muslin bag and hung up in the dairy. We always had a lovely ham for Xmas, as Mum's birthday was on 20th December, and mine on the 18th Dec: so we enjoyed it together. The ham had a different taste to that of today, as it was well matured, and without the injections and hormones of today, which make it grow fast but not to mature. From the pig, Mum made lots of 'pork cheese', a type of brawn, which was delicious.

As well as having scraps for tea with bread and butter, Mum made scrap pastries. The scraps were chopped fine, mixed with currants, peel and sugar, put in pastry, they made a very large pasty. She also made large apple turnovers, and we had them in the harvest field for 'fourses' , with a large pot of tea. As times got better we had meat on

Sundays. We had vegetable marrow pies, they were very tasty cut into small pieces, sugar put over them with large raisins (not the seedless kind). These would swell and were delicious with a short pastry crust.

We also had jam roly-poly, and for another favourite, summer pudding. Stale bread would be used to line a basin, soft fruit in summer and blackberries in autumn poured over, then a lid or plate put on weighted down, and left to stand overnight. Next day it would be turned out whole. We had hotpot with all sorts of vegetables, and all kept well and healthy.

My Mum churned her own butter, and when it was very hot in the summer time, and the butter would be too soft to pat up, the butter was put in the milk pail and lowered down the well until next morning. Mum would get up early and make it into ½ lbs. It would be very firm.

Granny Harriet Roberts

If we had a bad wound Granny Roberts would be sent for – she always brought her pot with her. She grew white lilies, collected the petals and covered them with brandy; the wound would be cleaned, a lily leaf put on the wound, and it was soon healed.

Granny Roberts also delivered most of the babies on Blackheath. As soon as Mrs. Gray at Hall Farm went into labour, they sent for Granny Roberts who nursed and looked after her. Mrs. Gray had 7 lovely boys, and a girl.

I reared all our ducks, chickens and turkeys. Before Xmas Mum would get lots of private orders, and all the rest went to the butchers. It was hard work plucking them all and getting them ready for the table. Mum and I were up until 3 o'clock in the morning, so we only had three hours in bed as Mum had to be up at 6 o'clock. Dad had to be up very early to give the horse a good bait before Mum drove to Lowestoft. I don't often have a chicken now, as I don't like the way they are reared in batteries, or the injections. I don't think they are healthy, and I like to see them running free, scratching for insects and basking in the sun.

When the ham was boiled, a lot of fat settled on the stock, when cold. Mum would take all this fat off and make ham fat cakes – they were delicious, made like a shortcake with a lovely flavour of ham. My daughter still talks of them, they were her favourite. My Mum had the most lovely set of teeth, they shone like enamel. Her customers often asked her if they were false. She never bought toothpaste or powder, but always cleaned them with soot and salt. I never knew her go to a dentist, and she had a full set of teeth when she died at 82 years.

Lowestoft was quite a long journey in a horse and cart – one of her customers who lived at the bottom of Nelson Street, was a boat owner's wife, Mrs. Catchpole. She was so pleased with her turkey, she invited Mum and I in, and gave us a glass of port wine and a mince pie. She asked Mum her name and when Mum told her 'Roberts' she said "What a lovely name, and what an honourable name, like Lord Roberts." She took my Mum's address. One year, we had a very sharp winter so Mum wasn't able to drive to Lowestoft, and Mrs. Catchpole wrote asking where she had been, and saying she missed her smiling face and cheery ways. Unfortunately that lovely house is now pulled down and made into a car park, and I believe it is now a supermarket.

We made all our own mincemeat, Xmas puddings and Mum made lovely home brewed beer for Xmas. When Dad had his corn threshed, Mum always brewed. She went to the Maltings at Halesworth, and bought the yeast which they used in the brewery to work the beer. Mum was always very worried when Dad had to take our horses to fetch the threshing machine from another farm, as our horses were not the heavy kind. She was always afraid they would strain themselves, but they never did. Mum was so thankful when the portable engine came.

Dad had to get several men to help thresh, and they were always very pleased to come as they liked Mum's home brewed beer. My brother and I were tee-total, so she made us 'hop-beer'. We grew our own hops which she used for the home brew, all the malt combs went to the pigs, nothing was wasted. We were never allowed to leave anything on our plates. If we did Mum would say "Waste not, want not, or you may live to say – Oh how I wish I had that crust which once I threw away." I often think of the waste of children today, and all the poor starving children of the world – I feel very strongly for them.

One Xmas Mum said it would be nice to make some 'fromerty' as it was such a very cold winter. She said she would need a bottle of rum to flavour it. We all shared in the cost, it was only 2/6 a bottle at the time, but that was a lot considering wages then. Mum soaked the wheat overnight, washed it and boiled it in milk, added sugar and some rum. It was lovely, we had it just before going to bed. We liked it so much, we bought another bottle of rum and had fromerty until the rum was finished. Xmas was the only time we ever had fromerty.

Ghostly Happenings

When the fishermen came home for Xmas, they went to my maternal grandmother's. She bought in a lot or oranges, and sold them. She also sold coal, kept pigs and sold pork, as well as the bread she made. These fishermen came round to the house and played with these 'twizzles' a large and a small one. They would buy the oranges to gamble with on the twizzles. Each would have a number and twizzle for them. The winner claimed all the oranges on the board. They went on until she had sold all her oranges.

Twizzle Boards

One night, the fishermen talked about ghosts, and one, whom they called Tilley, said he wouldn't be afraid of a ghost, he would go and shake hands with it etc. My Grandmother thought someone was stealing her coal, so she made a ghost dressed all in white and called it Elizabeth. She stood it just inside her coal house, and no more coal was stolen. These fishermen knew what sort of a man this Tilley was, so got my Uncle to put Elizabeth in the well lane, where Tilley would have to pass.

Tilley went home, and the others held back; all at once Tilley ran back, panting for breath and shaking like a leaf, saying there was a ghost in the lane. My Gran looked surprised, and said "A ghost." "That's right Missis, and it had got a bloody great mouth." It had been arranged for my Uncle to take it away while Tilley ran back, so they all went back with him asking where he had seen the ghost. "It was there, now it's gone," he said. I don't know if they ever told him the joke.

We played solitaire and all different card games.

Nine Men's Morris

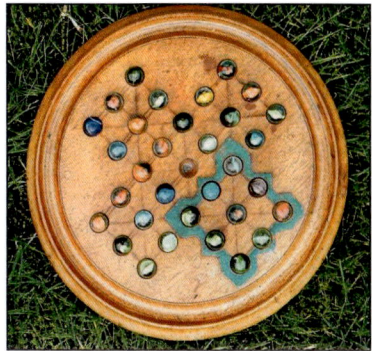

Solitaire

My grandfather was born exactly at 12 o'clock midnight, and he saw a lot which other people did not see. One day he had to take the cows to the marshes after milking, and went down Hog Lane at 8 o'clock. When he came back he told my Grandmother "I met Mrs. Gallon (he pronounced Girling this way) and I said "Morning, Mrs. Gallon."

She didn't take any notice, is she deaf or blind, she looked very funny about the eyes." Her son Fred lived in Hog Lane. My Uncle was an apprentice carpenter at Noy's of Bramfield. My Gran said "You're late home tonight." "Yes" he said "I have been helping to put old Mrs. Girling in her coffin, she died at 8 o'clock this morning." What my Grandad saw must have been an apparition.

When my grandfather was a boy, his father carted corn from one farm to another, and they were going down a very narrow lane. His father said "Boy, you have to walk behind the wagon, there's no room to walk on the side." When they got out of the lane my grandfather said, "Father, did you see that horse and coach with a man wearing a high hat, and carrying a whip, pass you?" His father replied "Boy, nothing could pass me, there wasn't even room for you to walk on the side." When they got home, he said to his wife, "What do you think this boy saw this morning?" When he told her about it she said she had heard the story before. My grandfather told me so many stories, these are the only two I can remember. My grandfather was one of the most trusted and truest men you could find.

My grandmother told me Albion House, in Wenhaston was haunted. It was very troublesome so they got the parson in who prayed "What troubles you?" It was bound down to a high hat and whip – the room was sealed off, and gave no more trouble. My Mum told me about Blythburgh Lodge being haunted. The farmer's daughter fell in love with a workman, and her parents tried to stop it, she was very unhappy. There was a very large pond at the back of the Lodge, and this young lady was seen walking around the pond with a Bible in her hand. It was laid down beside the pond, open with a verse marked which said "Why doest thou set watch over me" and she committed suicide in the pond.

My friend Elsie Freeman, whose Uncle Noah farmed Blythburgh Lodge, often stayed with her cousins there. One cousin, Elsie Etheridge, who was very fussy and folded all her clothes and laid them on a chair beside the bed, would find them thrown all over the floor in the morning. They said you would hear a noise like the rustle of silk, walking down the corridor.

My grandmother told me of an old lady known as a witch, who lived on the Heath. One day, an old gentleman rode past on his donkey, from Dunwich, to see some friends in Wenhaston. As he was going home this old lady stood by her gate. I don't know if he annoyed her in some way, but she said, "You'll fall off your dickey before you get home." This poor old chap was saying the Lord's Prayer all the way home, and he fell off his donkey just before he got to his gate.

Marriage, Children, More Visitors And A New House

After the first World War I got very friendly with Roland Ellis, always called 'Goldie' as he was very fair. His Dad was a builder, he had two brothers who followed the trade, but Goldie wanted to be an engineer.

Goldie as a little boy

His Dad took him to Leiston Garretts Works, and he was bound apprentice for five years. He only got 3/6 a week, his Dad paid for his board and lodgings, and he cycled home every weekend, which was eleven miles. The war was still on, and so when he was 17 years old, he broke his apprenticeship, and joined the Royal Air Naval Service.

After training in Sheerness and Crystal Palace, he was eventually posted to the Airship Station at Mullion, Cornwall, and later to Folkstone.

He flew 'Blimps' with a Rolls Royce engine fitted in an open suspended gondola. He had a course on Rolls Royce engines, and by this time he was flight engineer, and had logged 1500 flying hours.

Goldie in his Royal Naval
Air Force Service uniform

They flew the White Ensign while over water, and carried a Lewis gun, and two bombs. They maintained regular war time patrols north of Foreland, Calais, Colchester, Boulogne, Dieppe and Beachy Head. He remembered most the bitter cold, and encountering a floating mine.

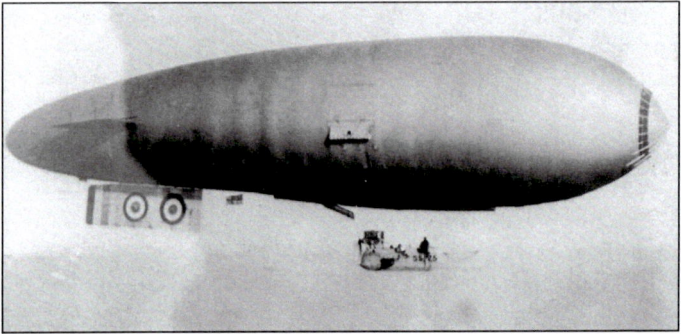

A blimp was a non-rigid airship with its engine fitted in an open suspended gondola.

Goldie was mentioned in dispatches and was awarded the oak leaf emblem.

Goldie logged 1500 flying hours in blimps. Once he descended through thick fog to ask two men leaning on a gate the way to Ashford.

The oak leaf emblem was worn with the ribbon of the Victory Medal and showed that Goldie had been mentioned in dispatches.

He was demobilized in 1919, and went back to Leiston Works to finish his apprenticeship and get his indentures.

The War of 1914-1918.

Royal Air Force

213086 A.M.1 R. V. Ellis

was mentioned in the London Gazette

dated 1st January 1919.

for gallant and distinguished services.

I have it in command from the King to record His Majesty's

high appreciation of the services rendered.

Winston Churchill

Air Ministry,
Kingsway,
London. W.C.2

Secretary of State for Air

He hadn't worked many months, when the firm had no more orders. Before the war Garretts sold steam engines to Russia. They were never paid for, mainly because of the Revolution there. After the war no orders, no work. He had to go on the dole with three waiting days with no money, then only for six months. After that a means test which he would not have. He did anything which came along, working on the farm pulling and topping sugar beet. After a time his father's bricklayer's labourer committed suicide so his father took him on at £2 a week.

Goldie bought a double dweller cottage (as they were called then). He gave £80 for it, hoping he could get possession. He applied for a grant, the council came and viewed it, and instead of getting a grant they condemned it, although the tenants were allowed to live in them for over 20 years, until they passed away. If we had the experience and courage of life, as we have had these last 60 years we would have told them what to do. We would have said "As you have condemned the cottages we consider they cannot be fit to live in. We will give six months notice to rehouse the tenants, after six months we will start to demolish them, clean the bricks and build a bungalow on the site."

We got married in 1926.

*Jessie and Goldie's wedding at
St. Peter's Church, Wenhaston.*

*From l to r. Percy Ellis (Goldie's brother), Goldie and Jessie.
The three bridesmaids were Maggie Mayhew, Beth
Hackwood and Sylvia Ellis, (Goldie's sister).*

Mum and Dad said we could have part of the farmhouse, but we decided to all live together. I paid for Goldie's board, and worked for my own living. I bought half an acre of land off the farm, for £15 which was a good price, as farm land was worth only £10 an acre at that time. We bought this, hoping one day we would be able to build a bungalow when we had saved enough money. I paid 15/- a week for Goldie's board, he had 10/- a week for pocket money and clothes. I had 15/- left which I tried to save each week. My aim was to save £100 each year.

My Mum gave me the 'attention' money when we had visitors, as they were getting better off, and had paid off all the borrowed money which they needed for valuation. Mum bought three cottages for £129, hoping to retire in one. She could never get possession, the tenants lived in them until they died.

I had a daughter in 1927. A friend bought me a lovely bunch of heather, picked from the common. We decided to call her Heather. When she was only a few weeks old, the first visitors of the year arrived. A Mr. and Mrs. North, two lovely small boys and a nurse. After they got settled in, they all seemed so happy. Mrs. North's solicitor was coming to stay for the week-end, as they were great friends.

Mum said "Oh dear, we must make another bedroom and toilet," as Ivy Cottage was especially for the family. Goldie said they could have his motor cycle shed which he had built, and he would put his cycle in the barn. We washed out the shed, painted the door white, and Mum said she had a nice commode she could put inside. Goldie asked Mum for a large piece of cardboard. After talking it over with Mum they agreed (both had a good sense of humour) to print the following on the card, as the visitor was a solicitor. "After a long and painful sitting, I thought I would let the matter drop." When the solicitor was introduced to his toilet he just roared with laughter, as this notice was hung on the wall above the commode. He invited all the family to inspect it, they really did enjoy the fun.

One morning the nurse came to Mum saying Mrs. North wouldn't get up; she suffered from depression, and the nurse wondered if Mum who was so full of ideas, could think of something to help cheer her up. I had cycled to Halesworth to do some shopping, and while I was away Mum thought of a good idea. When I returned she sprung a surprise on me.

She told me something had happened to Mrs. North (with whom she had already discussed the joke, and who was only too happy to agree). Mrs. North said she would like to see me when I returned, so I followed Mum into her bedroom. In bed was this handsome lady in a pure silk nightdress, lying in a large oak beamed bedroom with a lovely baby in her arms. I stood at the door in amazement. I didn't realise it was a joke. As I drew nearer, I shouted "It's my baby." I have never seen a more lovely picture, before or after. Mrs. North got up, all depression gone, the whole family were all so thankful, and the rest of the holiday was very happy.

Our next visitor was an artist, and his mother. Wenhaston was an artists' paradise, with all the lovely scenery, and the beautiful Blyth Valley. The artist was 'Allen Gwynne-Jones', who became a professor at Slade College University, London. He painted 'Wenhaston at Dawn' and 'Wenhaston at Sunset'.

At this time we had three running streams across the roads. 'Wenhaston at Dawn' was painted near Brook Farm. He got up at dawn, so I was up early to take him a cup of tea, and a jug of hot water. I left it on the landing, and knocked at his door. 'Wenhaston at Sunset' was down by the stream which divided Wenhaston and Thorington. They were two lovely pictures. I often wonder if they are still in England. I would love to see them again. The next time he came it must have been winter, as he painted 'The Dell' a small cottage on the marshes. It must have been nearly dark, as there was a light in the window and snow on the marshes.

On this occasion he had come to stay on his own, and when he returned there was a lovely fire in the parlour. When he came in he said "What a comfort." Mum had dished him up with a lovely partridge and vegetables for his dinner. The next day he said "You have looked after me so well, I would like to take you to the cinema in Halesworth." I said it was a very kind thought, and thanked him very much, but I must refuse. I went to all the whist drives in Halesworth and was very well known, so a young married woman going to the cinema with a single young man, would be remarked upon. At one whist drive after I had won 1st prize, a comment in the Halesworth Times the following week said, "Mrs. Ellis enhanced her reputation as a whist player." Mr.Gwynne-Jones promised me a small picture, but I expect he was too busy as it never arrived.

His mother decorated a beautiful jug and gave to me, I treasure it very much.

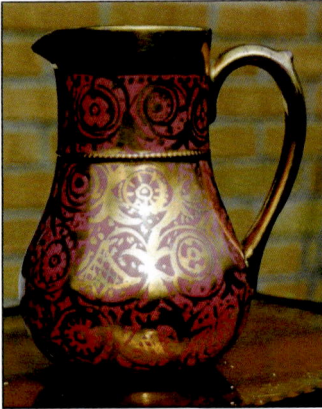

The jug decorated by Mrs.Gwynne-Jones. It is still in the family's possession.

The following year we had a very nice family, a Captain Lane who had been in the Navy. He came with his wife and son Michael. His son went to Wellington College, and on to Oxford University.

The Lane family's house in Milford-on-Sea. It later became a hotel.

During the Second World War, Captain and Mrs. Lane had retired, and had this beautiful house built at Milford-on-Sea, and when she heard the East Coast was being evacuated, Mrs. Lane wrote offering my children and myself a home. I appreciated the offer very much and thanked her, but I could not leave Goldie, and both Heather and Jack were at school, and we also had an evacuee, although she was the only one left from all the original evacuees.

Dear Goldie and Jessie,

This is my Church Tower. I am now Rector of St Michael on the Mount, Without in the middle of Bristol. I gave up being a Schoolmaster in July and was licensed in October in the Church on 1st October. We both are very happy about it. Next Summer (probably in May), we hope to make a tour of East Anglia including Kent so we expect to call on you then. I hope U. goes well. Michael and Patricia.

Thank you for your letter. I wish we travelled about more to see our friends; But we have such a full life in this Church that we don't get away much.

We must make a better effort this year o try to come East. Love to the Family.

Peace
and
Goodwill
to
you
this
Christmas
from
Michael and Patricia

St. Michael-the-Archangel-on-the-Mount-Without
Design by Marc Vyvyan-Jones. 1985
The Purchase of this card will help The Friends
of Bristol Radiotherapy Centre to finance
research and provide amenities for the patients.

Letter and card from the Lane Family

After we were married Goldie and I saw a bungalow in a builders magazine, which would cost £500 to build. This was in 1931, and as we liked the look of it, Goldie asked his Dad to build it, as they were very short of work at that time.

My son was born on 9th October, 1931. Goldie had been back on Leiston Works for about a year, but at this time he was stood off, as they had no orders. He had to go on the dole, and to have three

63

waiting days before getting any money. After a few weeks, he was called back again, an order had come in. It didn't last long as the firm went into liquidation.

After a very short time 'Beyer Peacock' bought the firm, as the country didn't look very rosy. Goldie was very quickly called back, as he was a wonderful tradesman. The firm started making guns for the navy; this would be about 1934. It looked as if there might be another war. The firm got very busy, and Goldie had quite a lot of overtime, which was a great help.

My father-in-law started digging the foundations for the bungalow, but he built quite a different one from that which we had chosen; he made all the rooms larger, and as it grew it looked very nice, and people said it looked like a gentleman's residence, in those days. Of course we thought he was doing it for the same price, so we didn't interfere. By the time it was half finished, he sent us a bill for £498. Of course, I naturally grumbled, but Goldie took it very calmly and accepted it. I didn't mind living with my parents for another five years, this was in 1931. I was very happy to stay at the farm.

All the time I helped on the farm, and earned my own living, and the children's. I was determined not to be defeated. My Mum was a wonderful and clever woman, who had a good sense of humour. She could tell us wonderful things of her life, which I wish could have been recorded. After the journey became too much for my Mum a Mr. Calver from Halesworth bought all our berries. He called me 'The Blackberry Queen' as I was the best and cleanest picker.

One day Goldie came home from the Works and said he was stood off as the firm was held up for material. I advised him to sign on for three days, which would be Wednesday, Thursday and Friday, but not to cycle through the village. Rather to go to Halesworth by Bramfield, the back way, to avoid going through the village street. He didn't take my advice. He went through the village and a very inquisitive resident asked him if he was going to sign on. Of course he said yes, so we went three days without any money. I wasn't allowed to earn anything, as Goldie had signed on, but I still went blackberrying as we had to live.

Would you believe this? When Mr. Calver's man called on the following Monday, he had sent a note by this man to Mum saying "Be careful, you have a friend. Clifford Goodwin the manager of the Labour Exchange, called and asked me how many blackberries I bought off Mrs. Ellis last week?" He had answered he had never bought any berries off Mrs. Ellis, which was true, because I was never there, he bought them all from my Mum and I always shared my earnings with her.

Goldie had a telegram on the Saturday morning, to start work first thing on Monday morning, and he was never on the dole again. People were very envious and jealous in those days, if they thought you could do better than them. My Mum, Mrs. Roberts', motto was "If you can't do anyone any good, don't do them any harm." Our son was named Jack Roberts as I wished. We had saved enough money to have the bungalow finished, Goldie did all the plumbing and lathing; we were very pleased as it had a fully timbered roof, and all the tiles were nailed on.

The bungalow was finished in 1936 and cost about £1000 with no entrance gates, and no toilet, so Goldie had to build one. It was a lot of money in those days, when houses could be built for £400 or even less. We moved in, on the first night we were there, Mum came to tea. I just sat and cried and Mum said "Don't cry, you have this lovely home and bungalow." Of course, I was missing the farm after forty happy years.

Wallace Ellis, who built the bungalow when he was younger.

Heather and Jack in the garden at Homeland

After Mum finished going to Lowestoft, she took her eggs, butter etc. to Southwold on the bus. The bus conductor was very helpful, and Mum made many friends. As time went on, she didn't feel like doing it any longer, so I went and enjoyed meeting all her very nice customers. I always went on a Wednesday as the auctions were held in the 'Crown Yard'. I always stayed and bought lots of furniture, I really did get some bargains.

At one auction Mr. Adnams Senr. who was the auctioneer, and knew me well as I was always there, brought on a large sideboard. It was a very nice one, but too large for most people. As the rooms at the bungalow were a good size, I knew it would fit in; my last bid was £4/10/- old money. Mr. Adams said he couldn't let it go for that, he would put it in the next auction. I knew I wanted that sideboard and must be at the next auction. The sideboard came up again, my last bid was again £4/10/-, he dwelt on it for a time, then agreed to let me have it at that price. I was thrilled, I knew I had a bargain although it was in a filthy condition.

At another sale, he finished the sale with two tennis net posts, marker and boundary fishing net; he couldn't get a bid. At last he said "Who will give me 1/-?" I very quickly put up my hand, and he said "Thank you, Mrs. Ellis." He was so pleased to get rid of the lot as everything had to be cleared from the Crown Yard that day. Goldie and I made a lovely tennis court on the paddock in front of the farmhouse. I didn't know much about tennis, but Goldie did as he played when in the Air Force. We marked it out, and bought rackets, and all had a very enjoyable time. It was a great attraction for the visitors.

The tennis court. Jessie is on the left, then Beth Hackwood, Lesley Brant, a local boy, and Marjorie Hackwood

I soon got settled down and was very happy. I went and helped Mum every day, and had dinner with them. Goldie worked very hard, overtime and weekends. He always had to clock on, if he was five minutes late when an apprentice he would lose half a day's pay. I never knew him to be late. When he went through Westleton, the people there called him 'The quarter to eight man' and timed their clocks. He was never paid for holidays, and we never had a holiday throughout his working life.

My son started school at 3½ years. The infant mistress agreed to take him on at so young an age. He had these lovely golden curls which I didn't want to cut until he was older.

The first year Jack was at school, he was given a very nice book at Christmas. The little boy who sat next to him in school didn't get one. Jack cried a lot and said "Mummy, can I give Colin my book?"

Jack aged three

I told him we shouldn't give away anything which is given to us, but I was going to Lowestoft the next day and I would buy a book for Colin and give it to him on the Monday. I always brought up my children to be kind to others. I was very happy to think Jack was so unselfish. The reason Colin didn't get a book was because years ago, a gentleman left a legacy for Wenhaston children only, and Colin came from Blyford; if I had been the teacher I couldn't have left the little boy out, I would have bought the book myself.

Wenhaston and Blyford United F.C. League Champions 1927-1928. Goldie's father Wallace is top right. Goldie is immediately below him.

Blackheath Farm about 1930.
Jessie's father is at the front, and Goldie is at the back of the cart.

1939, The Second World War, And The Years Since Then

Three years passed, then the Second World War broke out in 1939. Children were evacuated to Wenhaston from Essex, and everyone who had a house large enough had to take them in. The evacuees all arrived at the school, and there was a very nice girl who looked about Heather's age. Heather asked if we could take this girl who was with her mother and small sister. I didn't think we would be allowed any choice in the matter, but I spoke to the organiser and suggested if I took the girl, her mother and sister could go to Mum's at the farm. Although she looked to be Heather's age, she was in fact three years older, but short for her age so they looked much the same.

She hadn't the qualifications to go to the Grammar School where Heather attended, having won a scholarship to Sir John Leman at Beccles. I made an appointment to see the headteacher there, to see if Joyce might be allowed to go, but as the school she previously attended had not been a Grammar School, he had to refuse. She went to Halesworth Pupil Teachers' Centre and she was quite happy there although she didn't get the same subjects as she had followed at her old school – her French had to come by post, and the Maths were not quite the same, or perhaps not so many lessons. So I arranged with the Maths teacher at Halesworth to come Saturday mornings, and give her private lessons.

During the following year when the summer holiday came, her Dad arrived to take her home, as he explained, 'to get a job to help them out', he worked on the railway. She refused, but he insisted, and she sobbed all night. I told her Dad how she had cried, but he said tears meant nothing to him, and she was to go home. I told her the next morning that she would have to go home, as there was nothing I could do about it, but she wouldn't pack her case, she went home in what she stood in, and when she got to the gate, she ran back to say she would be back on Saturday.

The first year of the war was very quiet. When Joyce got home the bombing started, they almost lived in the air-raid shelter, and she carried on so much they were glad to send her back to us. In the meantime, the headmaster of Halesworth School brought her results of the summer examination, we were so pleased she had passed. In the spring I brought home two pairs of sandals for Heather to choose from; she fitted them on, one was expensive, the other a cheap pair. Heather asked if she could have the cheap pair so Joyce could have a pair too. I told her it was her choice, but how happy it made me feel that Heather was so unselfish.

Joyce wanted to go in for teaching, as that was what Heather wanted to do. By this time Joyce had got very friendly with my cousin's son, so that was another attraction. She stayed for another two years, joining the Young Farmers' Club, and the Youth Club, where Heather and Jack were already members.

The time had come for her to apply to College. I wanted her to apply for a college where she might get a scholarship. That was Bishops Stortford, but she didn't think she would be considered as she hadn't got matriculation. I told her I thought evacuation, and the good report from her headmaster would be taken into consideration.

On her birthday I opened a Post Office account in her name with 10/- old money. She did two days a week, pupil teaching, and was paid monthly, putting it straight into her Post Office account.

One morning a large envelope arrived for Joyce, and on opening it she found she had won a scholarship, so she was very excited, and we were all delighted. She stayed on getting everything ready for herself for College, she was always a very good, helpful and capable girl. She went home and wrote us a lovely letter which I treasure.

I treated her as my own daughter, and this is what she wrote.
Written on 22nd September 1942, when Joyce went to College.
Dear Mummy and Daddy,

It is easier for me to think about what I want to say than it is to write it down. What you thought of me when I left I cannot imagine, but I hope you will understand how I felt at that moment, I just couldn't say anything.

To merely say 'Thank you' for all that you have ever done for me, will never be sufficient. When I look back over the past three years, I realise that the way in which you took me, and made room for me in your house, is something very few would ever have done. Those who have never been away from their home may not imagine how much kindness has meant to me. Never have I felt an odd member of the family, and to think of the unselfish manner in which Jack and Heather accepted my presence, is admirable.

If ever I can do anything for any of you I shall be only too willing and pleased I can do something in return for the countless kindnesses which you have bestowed on me. Nevertheless, whatever I could do would never I am certain, repay the great debt of gratitude which I owe you all, with many sincere thanks,

Yours affectionately,
Joyce.

As she had long holidays, she stayed with us, going with Heather and Jack to help at the farm. She was still friendly with Geoff, who went into the Air Force for two years, and then on to College. Joyce passed out of College, getting a post at a Residential School. After Geoff passed out of College he joined Joyce at the same school. They decided to get married and wrote asking me if they could get married from our house, as they were her happiest days.

Joyce after she went to college

I was delighted to think they wanted this and readily agreed, asking how her Mum would feel about such a thing, but she replied that her Mum was delighted. We gave her a lovely reception at Homeland, and they had two children and have been very happy. They bought a lovely old cottage in Wenhaston and came to live there when the residential school where they worked, closed. Her first grandson was born on my birthday – I treat him as my adopted great grandson, and never forget his birthday.

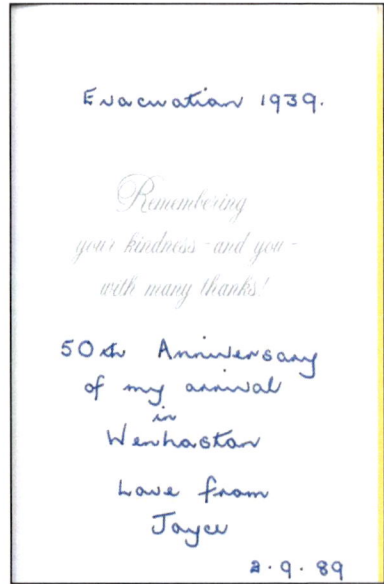

A card from Joyce, 50 years after her arrival in the village

Jack didn't pass his scholarship, so I made an appointment with the headmaster of the John Leman School to see if he would take him, as Heather was doing so well. He said I was being very naughty, as the entrance was on Tuesday. I replied that I thought he would pass his scholarship. The head said that one boy had passed his scholarship, but failed the entrance exam. Jack had to take some tests. I felt very shaky. He told me to come for him at 12 o'clock. I went back for him, and was told by the Head that he would let us know on Saturday if he had passed.

On Saturday I received a letter saying he had passed and would I get him uniform from Foster's of Beccles. We were all thrilled, but then I wondered where the money would come from to pay all his expenses, his bus fare to Halesworth, train fare to Beccles, school dinners, pocket money and above all, school fees and uniform, which would be about £30 a year; a lot of money in those days when Goldie's standing wage was only £2/12/- per week, with no holiday pay.

I decided to go pulling and topping sugar beet, but there was no machinery to pull and top at that time, it was very hard work. Mum said it would be best for me to take them so much per acre, and then I could come and go when I liked. I did this for six years, it was terribly hard work. Mum said if I was going to work so hard she would get me an insurance card and stamp it every week, so that when I was 60 years old I would get the state pension, that was my reward.

In May 1941 we were awakened at 4 o'clock in the morning with bombs dropping on the village. The next one landed in front of our bungalow; it was terrible after all the hard work and saving for ten years. We almost lost the lot. Goldie and I were in bed shaking like leaves.

Homeland before the bomb fell

I said to Goldie "We have had it," and waited for everything to fall in on us. We had Jack in our room on a small bed. He was 10 years old. His room was in the loft, but so many incendiary bombs had fallen on the field in front of the bungalow, we were frightened of fire.

The good work my father-in-law put into the bungalow saved our lives. The solid timbered roof lifted and went back down again with a bang. The noise was terrific, with everything landing on the roof. Every room was cracked where the plate of the roof lifted, you never saw such a mess. All the windows in the front were enclosed with galvanized frames, and blackouts made with sheets of galvanized iron, so the windows were protected.

Our lovely garden was absolutely buried. Goldie and I had walked round the garden the night before. I had said "Did you ever see anything more beautiful?" A rock garden all around the bungalow was in full bloom with all the spring flowers, and beds of tulips in the front lawn. We were heartbroken, but so thankful to think we were all alive. We had to have 500 tiles put on the roof, but no one was even injured. Joyce was still with us, all the evacuees were sent home, Joyce being the only one allowed to stay. Goldie took her to Saxmundham and persuaded the authorities to let her stay with us, so after a lot of discussion, they agreed.

The tennis court was all marked out, the family and friends had enjoyed themselves on the Saturday, just previous to the bomb falling at 4 a.m. on the Sunday. Not a flower or blade of grass could be seen. The hedge in front of the bungalow was completely buried; it was a 500 lb bomb, no one could ever imagine the damage. Although we had had to work hard and save for 10 years to build the bungalow, we were never bitter, only too thankful to be alive and well.

I have always believed in a supreme being who has watched and protected us all, and this was my third life saved.

We thanked my father-in-law for building us such a beautiful strong bungalow. We didn't have any more bombs in the village, but they were constantly dropping all around Lowestoft, Southwold and Leiston. Doodle bugs were constantly coming over, and we never knew where they would fall. We were all very thankful when the war was over.

B17s over Billingford by Joe Crowfoot.
The painting shows the contrast between the quiet
farming life in Suffolk and the bombers going over.
Copyright Joe Crowfoot

The Black Deek was destroyed in the war when the soldiers drove their tanks through and broke up the bottom. My parents told me it was a dew pond; lined with clay but it never held water after. Otherwise it was overflowing and provided water for thirteen Blackheath farm animals.

I was still very busy with the sugar beet as in those days there was no machinery to pull and top them. They lasted up to December, it got very cold and icy.

Jack's reports were not very good for the first year or so: it always said he had the ability but did not make the effort. Heather had wonderful reports, and grumbled at Jack saying, "Mummy is working so hard and you play about too much" – he was a happy-go-lucky boy, but after a time he worked very hard.

Heather took her School Certificate and got Matriculation exemption. Two years passed on in the 6th form, and then she went to St. Gabriel's College, Camberwell, London. The first year after the war we were still on rations. Heather wrote and said she was cold and hungry, and was writing in bed with gloves on! The heating hadn't been restored. We sent regular food parcels, and all the girls shared them together. I said I didn't think Heather would be homesick, although I could never go away from home on that account – I would rather work hard at home.

When Heather came home she brought a friend whose home was in Yorkshire. Her friend told us they were all homesick, but Heather had been the worst; she didn't want her Mummy to know. The heating was soon restored and they were all happy. When she went to college I opened an account at Lloyds Bank for her to pay all her expenses, as I knew she didn't like to write home for money. She could write out her own cheques, and she made the money last, never asking for more. I told her she had a bank account before her Mummy and Daddy. I was so pleased I had saved the money by the time she had to pay for her College fees.

Heather by the fish pond in the garden

After she got to College she sent me this little frame with these words beside the picture of a sweet little cottage.

What more could I have wished? I often read it and shed a tear.

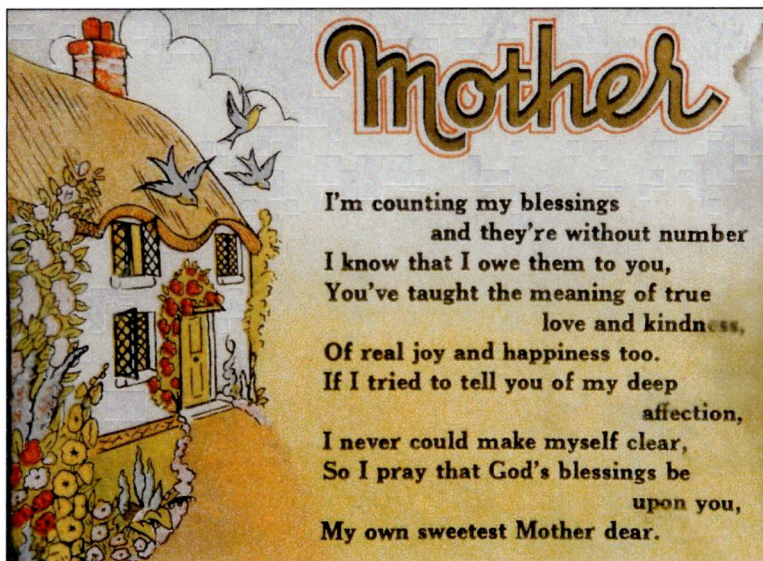

Mother

I'm counting my blessings
and they're without number
I know that I owe them to you,
You've taught the meaning of true
love and kindness,
Of real joy and happiness too.
If I tried to tell you of my deep
affection,
I never could make myself clear,
So I pray that God's blessings be
upon you,
My own sweetest Mother dear.

Heather passed out of college and got a post at an Ipswich school, coming home every weekend. She went to Ipswich by train, about 26 miles.

After her first pay packet she bought a bicycle, and cycled home to save her train fare. Goldie and I cycled half way with her when she went back, we were all very tired.

After a time, Jack got his School Certificate with Matriculation exemption. We all belonged to the Suffolk Naturalists Society (SNS) and still are members. This was a great help as they were both very good at Biology. When Jack went back to school after the summer holiday, he was to decide upon his future; you had to tell the Head what you wanted to do. Jack very reluctantly suggested teaching, but it was obviously such a reluctant choice on his part, the headmaster sent for me, as he wanted to know what he was most interested in; he didn't think he really wanted to teach. I told him Biology, but we felt there were not many openings in that field. The Head said he now knew which subjects he should follow, Biology, Chemistry, Maths and Physics.

After a time he was advised to apply for a County Major Scholarship. Jack was very interested in moths and butterflies and learnt a lot from the SNS as our friend Mr. Chipperfield was a treasurer for SNS and was an expert in this field. He had studied them for years and taken films. Jack reared caterpillars on a bramble, they were full and feeding. That morning he was going to take his first paper on Biology; he got to the gate, and ran back to see the exact colourings of the caterpillars. They were a lovely colour, he said, "You never know what questions you will get." When he came home he was so happy. He said "I had a gift, the life history of a moth or a butterfly." He had done the Emperor Moth.

He had applied to King's College, London University, as his first choice, but wasn't accepted at first. In his exam he got two distinctions and two 'A's and was awarded a State Scholarship, and a place at King's College. Just before the exam, the headmaster had told him he already had a County Major Scholarship. At that time they hadn't a Biology teacher at school, and Jack had to travel to Lowestoft Grammar School every Friday. He found it too much, leaving home at 7 a.m. to get to Beccles, and then on to Lowestoft, then a bus back to Southwold and wait for the bus to Wenhaston. By the time he got home at 7 p.m. he had a headache and couldn't do any homework, so he refused to continue in this way. A Mr. Kerr who worked at County Hall, was in the SNS and he was sent to Beccles every Friday, to take Biology lessons. He knew Jack very well, and brought him nearly home each week. Mr. Kerr told me afterwards, that Jack was the only boy in East Suffolk to get a State Scholarship. We were all delighted, as Jack had won a scholarship he was self-supporting.

After three years, he graduated and was able to go into research. He went to Manchester University to obtain his Ph.D. in strawberry research. After becoming an assistant lecturer, he was given a Fellowship to go to America, and later was selected to give a lecture at the International Congress of Genetics, in Montreal. He was given a Fellowship to continue research for a year, at Purdue University, Indiana.

When he returned he was looking for a job as his Professor Harland had retired from Manchester University. During the summer holiday, he had a very long wire from his Professor, asking him to meet Professor L. Penrose and himself, at University College, London. He quickly joined them in London, and was given a post working with Professor Penrose, on human cytogenetics.

Jack at his graduation

He had been working previously on strawberries. Later he went back to being a lecturer in plant genetics.

Fragaria Pink Panda
This is the ornamental strawberry plant
which Jack developed.

At Manchester University, he met a very nice girl who was one of his students. Her name was Valerie Hill, she graduated and was doing work for her Ph.D. In 1960 they got married.

Jack and Valerie's wedding
Goldie and Jessie are on Jack's left. Heather is far right.

They bought a house in Bourne End, Bucks. and have three lovely boys. Two are reading Marine Biology at Bangor University in Wales, and the eldest is at a Plymouth Polytechnic reading Environmental Science. Two hope to graduate in 1988. My son took early retirement at 54 years, although he still had a room at College as he had foreign students to finish their thesis for their Ph.D. He also did a lot of research at the Nuffield Foundation. He is now allowed to go there as a privilege because the mansion has been sold to an American millionaire. He has a Chinese student working there, to finish his studies for his Ph.D.

My son has bought our old farmhouse where he was born. I'm really thrilled he wants to restore it to some of its original beauty. He has had a greenhouse erected to help him continue his interest in plant breeding. He will do a lot of the work on the house himself, as he has been on a building course.

My daughter got married in 1955 to Peter Phillips, from Yoxford.

Heather and Peter's wedding
From the left, Elsie and Ted Phillips, Jack Ellis, best man, Peter
and Heather, Goldie and Jessie. The bridesmaids were Ann
Leech, Margaret Goddard and Christine Forsdick

She takes after my Mum, extremely capable and clever with her needle. They lived in one of Mum's cottages at first, which was very old, with lovely oak beams. We repaired and modernised it, and they lived there for five years. Afterwards they bought half an acre of land off the farm, and built a very nice bungalow facing the common, and named it 'Golden Acres'.

In 1972 we had another bungalow built at the bottom of our garden, as the original bungalow was now too large for us, and the new one was much easier to manage with central heating and no fires to be bothered with.

We celebrated our Golden Wedding in 1976. I prepared a lovely lunch for all the family, my daughter gave an evening meal for all the family.

We sold the old bungalow to a friendly lady, who seems to be almost one of the family, and a great asset to the village. Her name is Miss Eileen Snelling. She spent a lot of money in modernizing the bungalow with central heating and double glazing. She is very interested in nature, and keeps the garden and bungalow beautifully. We took the name 'Homeland' to our new bungalow, as it is my home, and I have lived on Blackheath since 1896.

My Mum developed chest trouble. Dr. Westhall got her into Southwold Hospital, as he thought I needed a rest. She didn't want to go at first, but after some persuasion got ready and looked forward to going. She had lunch, and when the ambulance arrived, the last words she said were that if I was unkind to Dad, she would never forgive me. Who would be unkind to such a loving Dad?

Mum was very happy in hospital, and told the patients all her life story. The patients and even Matron enjoyed my Mum's stories so much and laughed so much, that the next day Dr. Westhall told her she had done his patients more good than he had. Goldie's father's Christian name was Wallace. She told us to tell Wallace not to be afraid to come into Southwold Hospital, as everything there was lovely. Mum had a very bad attack and passed peacefully away in hospital at the age of 82 years.

My Dad came and lived with me, he had already had a few slight strokes, so often when I took his breakfast to him in bed, he couldn't speak and found it difficult to use his arm, but he soon got over them. He couldn't be left alone for long. One day I went to collect his pension. I had a lovely 6 pint electric kettle, which when it boiled whistled like an organ. When I got home I found he had filled it with coal, and put it on the fire. I said, "What have you done?"
He said in his Suffolk accent, "I hint done nothing." I hurried and emptied the kettle and filled it with water to wash it out, but the water

poured out as fast as I put it in. He had put it on the fire and burnt holes in it.

When Heather and Goldie came home and I told them what had happened, they both shook and roared with laughter. I felt more like crying, but you couldn't be angry with Dad, he thought he was being helpful. I had him for three years. One morning I didn't think he was very well. The Doctor called to see him, patted him on the shoulder and said, "You're a dear old chap." I sent for my sister-in-law, she told my brother he should go and see his Dad. In the evening we were all beside the bed. He shook hands with Heather, and with a twinkle in his eye said "Fare ye well." He shook hands with me and said, "You look well," shook hands with my sister-in-law, my brother and Goldie. He laid his head on the pillow, and at the age of 87 years, he passed away. Heather said, "Isn't death wonderful?" I said, "Not all are like that, he had been such a good kind man, trusting everyone, and as you live, so you die." My son wasn't there as he was at Manchester University. How my Dad adored Heather and Jack. Heather was at the farm for the first ten years of her life, and spent so much time with her Grand-dad. Jack was six years at the farm. We were all so happy, and so sorry to lose him.

This kindness went on for three generations. During the time the railway was being built, my great grandfather called George Clark, lived near the Toll House, at Mells near Halesworth. He met a Mr. Lansbury (who was working on the railway) and his pregnant wife, looking for lodgings. He said "I'll find you lodgings in the toll house," so Mr. and Mrs. Lansbury lodged there. My great grandmother nursed her, delivering her of a boy. My great grandfather asked what they planned to name the baby, and they said "George, after you." He must have been very clever, for after many years he became a Member of Parliament, and was the George Lansbury, Leader of the Labour Party. The Toll House was very small but large families lived in small houses in those days. One part of Halesworth today, is called 'Lansbury Road'.

My great grandfather was registered as Robert, but was always known as George. His first grandson was named George, and his second grandson Robert, who was my Dad.

When I was 60 I got the State Pension. After 2½ years I had saved it all, which was £2/10/- per week. This was the end of 1959, and although he was by now foreman of his shop at the Leiston Works, I suggested to Goldie that he should retire, as we could manage for another 2½ years until he drew his State Pension, as he would get no pension from his firm. His wage was somewhere between £7-£8 per week, less travelling expenses, wear and tear on clothes etc. I thought he had worked long enough all through the cold winters, in the cold workshops.

After the Christmas holidays, he made arrangements with the headmistress of Wenhaston School, Mrs. Jackson, to take the children for their nature lesson on wild flowers and birds. He took them on all the footpaths, so they should be remembered, as he was very keen to keep all the footpaths open for future generations. He always inspected the footpaths before he took the children, and always took shears with him in case brambles should be in the way. He would check to see if the bridges were safe, and took a piece of carpet in case of barbed wire, so the children would not tear their clothes. This he enjoyed doing very much until his death at 86 years.

When I was 85 I had a bad fall, hurting my thigh, but still I kept going. My own Dr. Hopkins was on holiday, a Dr. Drain came and wanted me to go to Lowestoft Hospital for an Xray. I had great difficulty in walking, but when I got to hospital two nurses undressed me, and a very nice doctor examined me. He didn't think I had broken anything and didn't need an Xray. Although the nurses helped me, getting dressed again was an ordeal. I was just going home when Dr. Drain insisted I had an Xray. I had to get undressed again, had the Xray, but still they couldn't find anything wrong. Everything at home carried on as before for a few days; I prepared dinner for all the family, and all were seated at the table waiting for me to join them. I managed to get as far as the dining room door, when my right leg seized up, and would not move at all. This was on the Monday, my son-in-law and Goldie went to Southwold to the Red Cross, and got me a wheelchair, so Goldie pushed me around the garden. This went on until the Thursday, when I was feeling very bad.

My daughter phoned the doctor, my own doctor still being on holiday. A very nice young doctor came, who was Dr. Hopkin's future son-in-law. When he saw my leg he looked very grave, and said he would have to have further advice. He talked to my daughter for some time, and when she came in she told me the doctor was sending me to hospital, and it would be better to get undressed just in case.

My son and his family were staying at the farm, and were spending the evening at my daughter's. My eldest grandson was already there. The telephone rang, it was the doctor saying he had got me a bed in Heathrow Hospital, Ipswich. This was at 7.45 p.m., the ambulance was due at 8 p.m. My grandson hurried to the farm, where he found my son having a bath. They all hurried to our bungalow just in time to see me on the stretcher, being lifted into the ambulance. All the family followed on to Ipswich. A very nice Dr. Hughes said my doctor had been right as I had 'thrombosis' and it was very urgent. I was connected to a machine by my wrist, and laid on my back. After I was settled, he invited all the family in, and a large pot of tea was ordered for all. I was given tablets and had the best night's rest for three weeks.

Next morning, Dr. Hughes brought a specialist in to see me, and introduced me as a fine example of a true 'East Anglian'. I felt very proud, I loved our accent. Both my parents, my husband and two children and myself, were all born in Wenhaston. My Dad's accent was lovely. He didn't say Southwold – it was Seffold. Walberswick was Walserwig. 'Hi in the hol bor, hinder comes a dow' translated would be 'Hide in the ditch boy, yonder comes a pigeon'.

Although I was Xrayed nine times they could not decide what was wrong with my thigh. One doctor thought it was chipped. A specialist came one day and help me to walk down the ward. He told me at last he had discovered it was cracked, and very difficult to find. Dr. Drain had been right when he insisted on that original Xray in Lowestoft. I consider that my fourth life was saved by a clever young Dr. Huggins who got me into Ipswich hospital so quickly. He is now a surgeon.

When I was 80 years old I was given an extra 25p to my State Pension. I thought it was given to all those who worked and served their country in the First World War. Whichever Government has been in power, not one penny had been added to that 25p, although inflation went sky high. We are the forgotten few.

I have told how I worked on the land during the First World War, and how my brother who is 92 years old, was mate on a drifter and went mine-sweeping. My favourite cousin Bob, who is 96 years old, was a skipper on a drifter and also went mine-sweeping.

After he retired he lived in Benhall, and often went gardening at Lady Penn's house in Sternfield. The Queen Mother often stayed there. During the 1914-1918 War, when George V1 was Prince, he met Bob when they were training. One day at Sternfield, the Queen Mother went into the gardens and said "Are you the Bob my husband used to talk about?" "I'm him," said my cousin, and she went to shake hands with him. Bob said "My hands are too dirty." "Oh, " she said, "it's true English soil" – What a wonderful lady. My son-in-law's mother is 94 years old, and is another wonderful example to the present generation.

As I was about to finish my story I had a very bad fall, and broke my hip. I was taken into Gorleston Hospital and had an operation. After ten days I was transferred to Patrick Stead hospital at Halesworth, to be near my family and friends. I was in hospital for seven weeks, and was over-whelmed with kindness from the doctors, nurses, family and friends. I am now home, my daughter Heather who lives in a lovely bungalow next door to me, treats me with the greatest kindness, altogether better than being in a first class nursing home, as I am in my own home.

I have an excellent home-help, which is a great comfort. Apart from being near to death on four occasions, I have had a broken rib, a cracked thigh, a broken hip, two broken wrists, and fluid taken off both knees. I have had hepatitis, thrombosis, and two bad attacks of bronchitis and here I am at the age of almost 92 years, feeling so grateful that I have the ability and memory to write this long story.

I feel I have always had a friend who protected, guided and watched over me, and that friend is Jesus.

I would like to end my story with my favourite hymn, 'What a friend we have in Jesus' very kindly sung by a dear friend – Mrs. Betty Best,

Thank you, Betty.
Betty, who became Mrs. Hatcher, sang this hymn at Jessie's funeral.

*Jessie on her 90th birthday
with Heather and Peter*

Appendix - interesting words used by Jessie

p.8   Egg and bacon flower – water crowfoot
Black Deek – deek is an old word for ditch, although this was actually a pond. It was used as a watering hole by farm animals from around the common. Manoeuvres in World War 2 broke the bottom up and it never held water properly afterwards.

p.22   Slops – clothes worn by fishermen

p.26   Haysel - haymaking time
Gavel - to rake mown hay or barley into rows ready for carting. A shock was an arrangement of sheaves, set up endwise in the field to dry. In some counties this was called a shook.

p.29   A governess cart was a small two wheeled cart usually drawn by a pony.

p.41   A dorothy bag was a bag with handles. They were usually made from cloth, but Jessie's were made with rushes.

p.42   Buskins were half boots, rather like gaiters.

p.43   'Clog' wheat – bearded wheat.
Corn cockle. A pink or purple wild flower, pretty but with poisonous seeds. It was common but it is now rare.

p.44   The fishermen always caught herrings at the home fishing.

p.45   Pigs fry is a dish featuring the cheaper but tastier parts of the pig. It included scraps of pork meat such as pork belly mixed with various pieces of kidney, liver, heart, lights (lungs) and sweetbreads and onions. Fat which looked like lace was carefully spread over the top. When it melted it helped to make a lovely rich gravy.

p.45   Warmed our crops – warmed our insides.

p.46   Fourses – refreshments at 4 o'clock.

p.49   Malt combs (or cooms/culms) – the refuse from the malt after brewing

p.51   Jessie's grandfather was born at 12 midnight. These are called the chiming hours and those born at this time are thought to have special powers.

p.53   Dickey – Suffolk dialect for donkey.

p.57   Double dweller – a semi-detached cottage.

Before 1971, money was divided into pounds (£), shillings (s. or -/-) and pennies (d.)
There were 20 shillings in a pound, and 12 pence in a shilling.
A guinea was 21 shillings (£1/1/-)

Volume

8 pints in a gallon
2 gallons in a peck
4 pecks in a bushel. Bushels were usually used in agriculture

Jessie's Ginger Biscuit Recipe

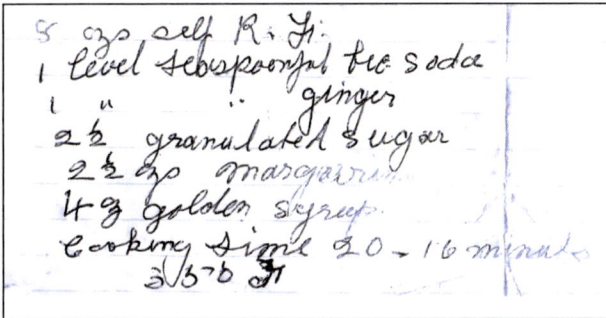

8 ozs self R.F.
1 level teaspoonful bic soda
1 "   "   ginger
2½ "   "   granulated sugar
2½ ozs margarine
4 oz golden syrup
Cooking time 20-16 minutes
350° F

Happy memories of the Primitive Methodist Chapel.

I was born in a sweet little cottage, surrounded by common land, covered with beautiful heather & gorse. Almost on our door step was the Primitive Methodist Chapel. When I was old enough I was sent to Sunday School morning, afternoon & to the evening service. I had an Uncle whose name was Harry Self, he was partly crippled with frost bite when young. Most Sundays we had local preachers, one was a lady Mrs Cordle, & I remember her text so well, it was taken from Joshua, "As for you & my house we will serve the Lord". One Sunday a Mr Holmes preached, he was very slow & boring, his text was about selfishness, after a long pause he shouted, is there a Mr Self in this house. Poor old Harry, who always sat at the back of the Chapel near the tortoise stove which was very easy & most of the congregation turned & looked at Harry. One Sunday I wasn't preaching, he was looking to see if old Holmes was preaching, if so I aint going, I just show how careful & tactful one have to be when preaching from the pulpit. In the early summer we had a camp meeting, lot of the forms were taken from the Chapel & put near the Black Dyke, which I was covered with a lovely small flower yellow & white we called it egg & bacon, around the pond was maiden hair & ox-eye daisies & the scent from the gorse was lovely. My Dad took his Waggon onto the common for the service to be conducted from. We had lovely Sankey hymns

One of the passages which Jessie wrote, reduced a little in size.
Her writing just flowed, without the use of paragraphs.
Her handwriting was very good for someone aged over 90.

Sampler made by Eliza Read, Jessie's grandmother in 1838.
She was brought up in Bramfield, a village near Wenhaston, and
made the sampler there.

The verse at the end reads:-

Learn to condemn all praise betimes
For flattery is the nurse of crimes
With early virtue plant thy breast
The specious arts of vice detest.

Jessie's Family

Eliza Read
1831-1916

m.Simon Goddard	George Spindler	m.James Spoore
1820-1866	1832-1917	1822-1909
Married in 1855		Married in 1889

Simon died of consumption, leaving Eliza with three children aged 4, 7 and 10, and 22 acres of land to farm. George Spindler was employed to help her farm the land. Eventually they lived together and had two children, Jane (Jessie's mother) and James. They considered marrying but did not. Eliza visited a fortune teller, who told her not to marry him. In 1889, when Jane was 19, they both married someone else.

Eliza's children with Simon

Eliza's children with George

Fred	Mary Ann	George	Jane Goddard	James Goddard
1855-1910	1858-1889	1862-1943	1871-1952	1872-1948

Fred died in Bulcamp workhouse. He was there in the 1901 census, as a wheelwright. He may have gone there because he was blind with cataracts.

Mary Ann married Harry Self 1853-1911

Anna Elizabeth	Ellen Louisa (Nellie)
1885-1968	1887-1950
married James (Tom) Mayhew	married Charles Day

Tom	Maggie	Daisy	Connie

Anna lived with her father and step grandfather James Spoore after her mother died in childbirth, but she was mainly brought up by Jane and Robert Roberts, Jessie's parents.

Ellen lived with her aunt and uncle in Westhall, then in Carlton Colville.

Harriet Clarke (Granny Roberts)   married   Robert Roberts
1836-1925   1858   1837- 1913

They had 5 children including Robert, Jessie's father.

Their son Harry, 1875-1918, died in the First World War and is named on Wenhaston War Memorial.

Jane Goddard   married   Robert Roberts(Snotcher)
1871-1952   Christmas Day 1894   1870-1955

    | |

James   Jessie Emmeline m. Roland Victor Ellis (Goldie)
1895-1989   1896-1991   1897-1983
                married in 1926

Goldie's parents were Wallace (a builder) 1868-1952
and Kate 1870-1951

    | |

Heather m. Peter Phillips   Jack Roberts m. Valerie Hill
                        | | |
                     Matthew Timothy   James

Jane and Robert Roberts in 1948 at Blackheath Farmhouse